PHOTOSHOP Retouching Cookbook
for Digital Photographers

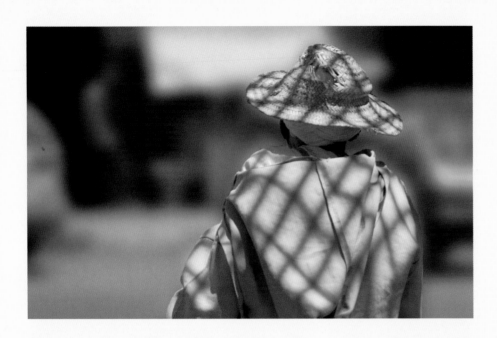

PHOTOSHOP Retouching Cookbook
for Digital Photographers

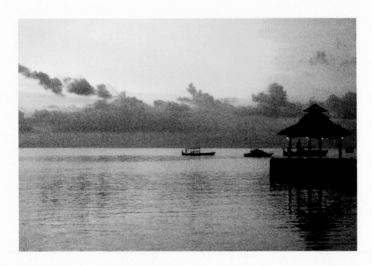

Barry Huggins

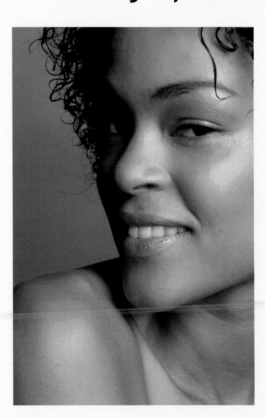

O'REILLY®

First edition for the United States, its territories and dependencies,
Central and South America, and Canada published in 2005 by O'Reilly Media, Inc.

O'Reilly Media, Inc.
1005 Gravenstein Highway North
Sebastopol, CA 95472
USA
www.oreilly.com

Editorial Director: *Edie Freedman, O'Reilly Media*
Cover Designer: *Edie Freedman, O'Reilly Media*

The O'Reilly logo is a registered trademark of O'Reilly Media, Inc.

O'Reilly books may be purchased for educational, business, or sales promotional use.
For more information, contact our corporate/institutional sales department:
(800) 998-9938 or corporate@oreilly.com

Downloadable image files of the examples in this book can be found online at:
http://examples.oreilly.com/photoretouch

International Standard Book No. 0-596-10030-2

This book was conceived by:
ILEX, Cambridge, England
www.ilex-press.com

ILEX Editorial, Lewes:
Publisher: *Alastair Campbell*
Executive Publisher: *Sophie Collins*
Creative Director: *Peter Bridgewater*
Managing Editor: *Tom Mugridge*
Editor: *Stuart Andrews*
Art Director: *Tony Seddon*
Designer: *Ginny Zeal*
Junior Designer: *Jane Waterhouse*

ILEX Research, Cambridge:
Development Art Director: *Graham Davis*
Technical Art Director: *Nicholas Rowland*

For more information about this title, please visit:
www.web-linked.com/cretus

Manufactured in China

9 8 7 6 5 4 3 2 1

Contents

INTRODUCTION

Selections

Layer Masks

Clipping Masks

Introduction

Over the past decade, the digital revolution has affected us all, changing our everyday lives in a thousand small but significant ways. Computerization continues to have an impact on everyone, regardless of generation, gender, or our own technophilia or phobia. There is scarcely an element of our existence that is not influenced in some way by the microchip, from the way we work to the way we play, how we communicate and shop, the flow of our finances, our methods of learning, and even simply moving from A to B.

Photography has not been left unscathed by this digital invasion. In fact, it has seen some of the most dramatic alterations. The traditional wet darkroom—the esoteric preserve of the professional and keen amateur photographer—now teeters on the edge of obscurity, its arcane practices consigned to dusty volumes for posterity.

Today, a new "digital darkroom" heralds a utopia for anyone interested in creative photography. Whether you are a professional, an amateur, or somewhere in between, this book has been written to demonstrate how you can use an industry-standard image-editing application to retouch your photographs with a power and flexibility that goes beyond what even experts could achieve in the old-fashioned wet darkroom. Using Adobe Photoshop, the choice of professional retouchers and graphic designers, you'll see how to add a professional finish to your photography—touches that can often be the difference between a winning image and one consigned to the bottom drawer.

Digital photography is a great medium, but it does have some limitations. It won't enable you to recompose a shot or bring the sun out from behind a cloud or brighten the red paintwork. And it definitely won't prevent the unsuspecting tourist from walking into frame just as Krakatoa is erupting. However, using Adobe Photoshop, we can resolve all these problems, plus a myriad other irritating situations that can render your image a failure.

Color correction and creative color manipulation are the mainstays of photographic post-production. Along with brightness and contrast adjustments, and the general control of light, this area is probably the most intensively worked element of the digital darkroom. As anyone who has ever attempted to recover an image from the depths of darkness or revitalize a washed-out image will attest, the prescribed solution is not always successful. One size definitely does not fit all when it comes to digital manipulation. As a result, this Cookbook covers a variety of "recipes" that should take care of most scenarios. By engaging in a little creative mixing of techniques, only the most under-performing image will be headed for the trashcan.

If color and brightness/contrast editing are the bread and butter of digital manipulation, then the crème brulée has to be special effects: the subtle reflection that would have stopped Monet in his tracks and implored him to commit it to canvas; the strategically placed blur that renders the subject almost three-dimensional against a distracting background; the suggestion of fluid motion left by a ghostly trail in the moving subject's path. All these tricks will be added to your collection.

We can also take a second look at some traditional wet darkroom techniques, as many can be replicated in digital form. Techniques such as film grain, a favorite tool of many photographers to invoke a certain mood. Reticulation and mezzotints both exist as standard Photoshop filters, but in keeping with our theme of multiple recipes, we'll also outline a more customized approach. Solarization, a haunting and enigmatic style embodied famously in the work of the surrealist artist and photographer Man Ray, is covered, using an unusual approach that allows you tremendous scope for creative transformation. Infrared photography was traditionally the domain of the scientist, but now this compelling photographic style is easy for anyone to mimic.

Arguably the most commonly photographed subject is the human form itself—and perhaps no other subject is more prone to criticism. Here you will learn how to construct the essential elements of the cover girl shot, from whitening teeth and eyes, and removing wrinkles and skin blemishes, to enhancing lips and skin tone, sculpting the face, and even changing hair color.

On a more functional note, you will be guided through the techniques of creating strong black-and-white and color-tinted imagery—a function omitted from many digital cameras. We'll also look at removing unwanted elements from your photographs, whether it's people in the background or a stray speck of dust. And if you have valuable, irreplaceable images that have been damaged by age or poor storage, we'll show you how to fix these too.

Though the emphasis is on updating old photographs and cleaning up imperfect ones, we'll also run through some recipes designed to make you equally adept at doing the reverse: simulating an antique photograph, resplendent with fading, cracks and all the telltale signs of advancing years. In a similar vein, your photographs can be turned into classic prints using a range of posterization techniques.

Finally, for anyone seriously delving into the hidden power of digital photography, we will take a tour into the RAW format—the digital equivalent of the negative. Using Photoshop's camera RAW plug-in unleashes a powerhouse of adjustments, enabling you to not only perfect your image prior to opening it in Photoshop, but also helping you to rescue detail which may otherwise be lost.

Whatever your level of expertise, working through the recipes in this book or just using them as the basis for your own experimentation will help you come a step closer to what we all dream of: the perfect picture.

Barry Huggins

Throughout this book, we'll be doing some work that involves adjusting or transforming isolated elements within an image. Every Photoshop artist has his or her own favorite methods of selection, but they all have their place and their uses.

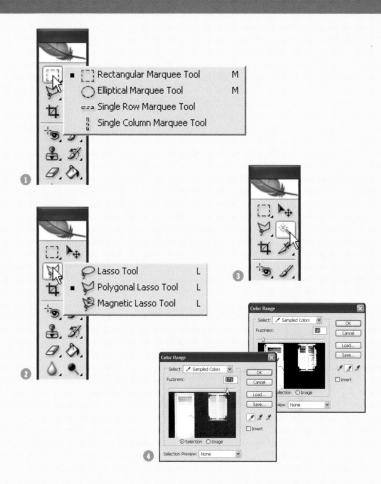

① THE MARQUEE TOOLS

Ideal for selecting regular areas, including windows and doors with the rectangular Marquee, or irises and pupils with the elliptical Marquee. The single line Marquees are useful for adjusting existing selections or removing a single line from an image or a layer. To select a perfectly circular or square area while using either the elliptical or rectangular Marquee, hold down the Shift key as you drag it out. To drag out from a central point rather than the edge, hold down the Alt/Opt key. To do both, hold down both keys.

② THE LASSO TOOLS

With a graphics tablet and a steady hand, the freeform Lasso can be an excellent tool for making rough selections. Otherwise, the polygonal Lasso is ideal for isolating simple shapes, or complex ones provided you have the patience to make a lot of anchor points. If the edge of your object gives you some contrast to work with, the magnetic Lasso can also make extractions very easy. You can switch quickly from the Magnetic Lasso to the Polygonal Lasso by holding down the Alt/Opt key, then clicking. This is a useful trick if your selection loses its edge for a small section, giving the Magnetic Lasso very little to work with.

③ THE MAGIC WAND

As with the Polygonal lasso, the Magic Wand works wonders where there is a clear edge and plenty of contrast: it can be a great tool for removing backgrounds from a shot or selecting cutouts. The Magic Wand and the related Color Replacement tool are designed to select areas of a specific color in the image. However, by checking or unchecking the Contiguous checkbox, you can define whether it confines the selection to adjacent pixels within the Tolerance range, or whether it picks all colors in the image within the Tolerance range. This can be useful if, say, you wish to select a sky behind the branches of a tree, though in some of these cases it may be wiser to switch to the Color Range command.

④ COLOR RANGE

An undervalued selection tool, the Color Range tool (**Select > Color Range**) works well, as you might expect, for selecting areas of a particular color or tone. You can use the standard, plus, and minus eyedroppers to select a hue, then increase or decrease the range of colors affected. Alternatively, you can make a basic selection, then move the Fuzziness slider up and down. As with so many of Photoshop's tools, experimentation will help you master the tool and its uses.

SELECTION TIPS:

• It's useful to be able to build up one selection from multiple selections, and Photoshop gives you the tools to do just that. You can add to the current selection, subtract from the current selection, or intersect two selections in two ways: by clicking the buttons on the left-hand side of the Tool Options bar, or by holding the relevant shortcut key having made one selection, and then making the next. Hold Shift to add to the selection, Alt/Opt to subtract from the selection, or Shift + Alt/Opt to intersect two selections. You can change selection tools between selections as you go, enabling you to combine selection tools for best effect.

• The Quick Mask is a great way of tightening up a basic selection. Make a start using the standard selection tools, then select Quick Mask mode (the right button of the two beneath the Foreground and Background Color swatches). Use a small brush to paint with white to add to the selection, and black to subtract from it. Click the Standard Mode button to finish.

• You can always save a selection for later use. Choose **Select > Save Selection** to transform the selection into an alpha channel.

9

LAYER MASKS

Layer Masks are another Photoshop feature that we'll use extensively in this book. As you're probably aware, Photoshop enables you to build composite images using layers. Adjustments or selected portions of an image can be assigned to a layer, which can be made more or less transparent using the Opacity slider. The order of the layers can also be rearranged by moving them up and down within the Layers palette, and the ways in which the layers interact with each other can be changed using the Blend drop-down menu. Changing these blending modes can have dramatic effects, as we'll see later on.

Layer Masks enable you to easily customize which parts of a layer are visible, hidden, or partially visible. In this example, the bottom layer is a full-color shot of a window in a hotel bedroom. The top layer is the same shot, desaturated. By adding a layer mask (the easiest way is to highlight the layer, then click the third button from the left at the bottom of the Layers palette), we can paint over the window in black to let the color window below show through. Painting on white restores visibility to the layer, and painting in gray enables you to do the same at varying levels of opacity, depending on the strength of the tint. This becomes particularly useful when creating compositions or when tweaking the effect of a strong image adjustment.

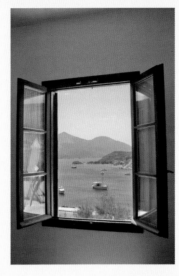

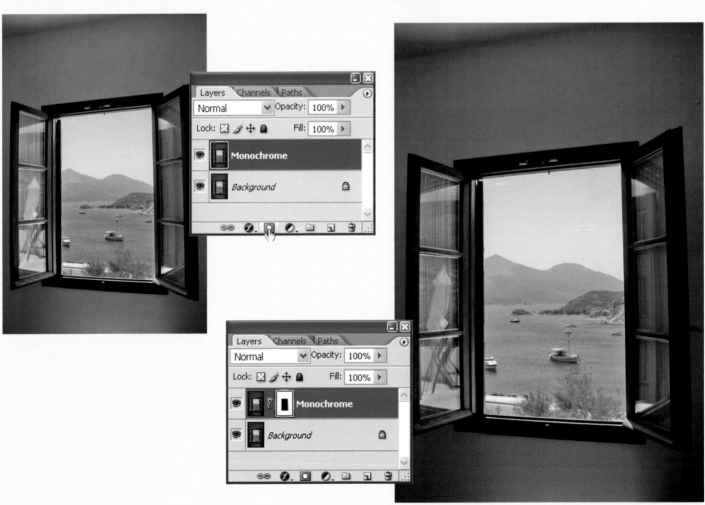

CLIPPING MASKS

Clipping Masks use the content of one layer to mask the layers above it. A shape or a logo on one layer will allow the contents of the layer above to show through. This has a multitude of uses, and we'll explore some of them in projects later on. This is just a simple demonstration. On the bottom layer, we have a straight studio portrait shot. On the top layer, we have the same shot, inverted. In the middle is a simple black box (with a drop shadow and stroke layer style added for effect—don't worry about these for now). Clicking the middle layer, holding the Alt/Option key, then hovering on the line between the top and middle layers will bring up a special "create clipping mask" pointer. Click again to create the clipping mask.

As you can see, the middle layer now acts as a mask, hiding most of the top layer except for the portion in the black box. Note that moving the box changes the portion of the layer revealed. This technique opens up a multitude of other effects.

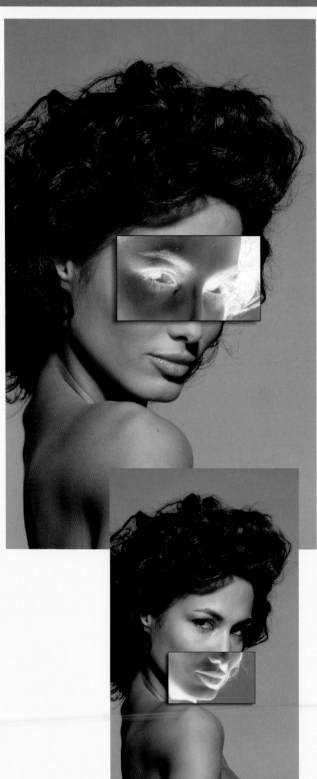

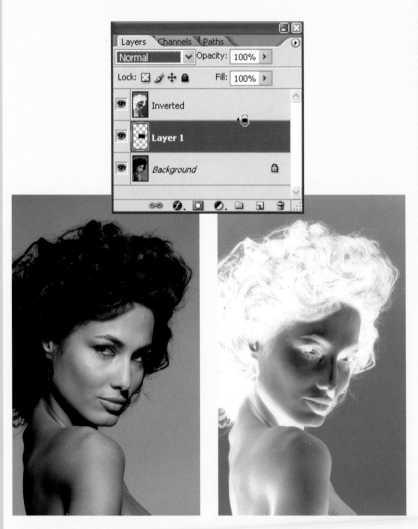

EXPOSURE CORRECTION

Correcting over- and underexposure

Controlling contrast

Difficult exposure problems

Correcting over- and underexposure

Most photographers, whether amateur or professional, would put over- or underexposure at the top of their list of reasons to reject an image. However, some of these images can still be saved. With a few simple adjustments from Photoshop's impressive arsenal of tools, washed-out photos can be rescued from the scrapheap, and gloomy shots brought into the light of day.

Method 1: **Brightness/Contrast**

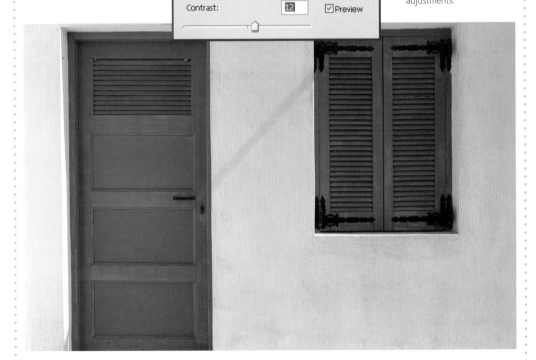

1 We'll use the simplest of all brightness adjustment tools on this underexposed shot. Go to **Image > Adjustments > Brightness/Contrast.** The controls are pretty straightforward: drag the Brightness slider to the right to increase brightness.

2 However, as brightness increases, contrast will start to decrease. To compensate, drag the Contrast slider to the right to match. This tool is fine for simple tasks, but it's not very flexible. All pixels are brightened by the same degree, which causes problems in more complex images where different areas require different adjustments.

Brightness/Contrast

Brightness: 31

Contrast: 12

OK
Cancel
☑ Preview

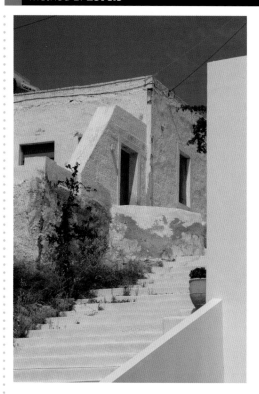

Most Photoshop professionals will ignore the Brightness/Contrast command and reach for the Levels tool instead. The palette gives you a histogram of the tonal levels within the image, with sliders at the bottom to control the white, black, and gray (or gamma) points. In this example, the white stonework against a bright sun causes all sorts of problems for the camera's auto exposure systems. The camera over-compensates, resulting in a dark image.

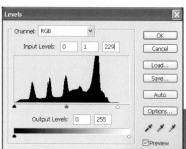

1 Press Ctrl/Cmd + L for levels (Image >Adjustments > Levels). Our image is too dark, so we'll leave the black slider alone—but notice how far to the right the white slider is positioned. Drag the white slider to the left to a value of about 229—the point where the histogram graph begins.

2 The gray slider in between the white and black sliders adjusts the gamma point. By shifting this, we can make fine adjustments to the brightness without dramatically affecting the extreme light and dark areas of the image. Drag the gamma point to the left to brighten the midtones, or to the right to darken them. Here we make a small adjustment to the left to introduce a little more light.

Tip

For a quick Levels adjustment, try Image > Adjustments > Auto Levels. This can be an effective tool, or offer a point of comparison for your own, more controlled Levels adjustments.

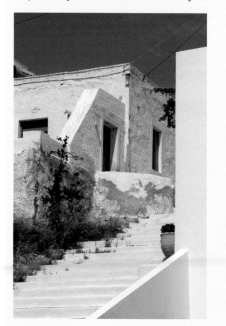

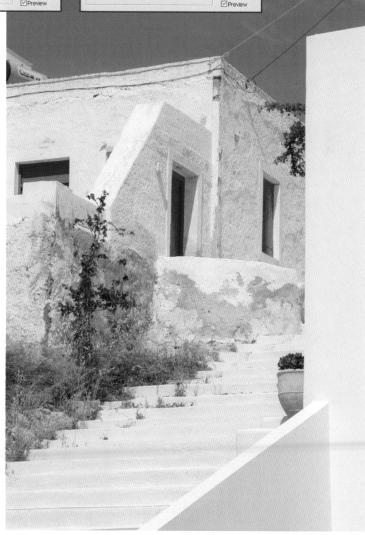

15

Correcting over- and underexposure

Method 3: **Curves**

Sometimes Levels doesn't work effectively, and then it's time to wheel out the big guns: Curves. This image suffers from overexposure in the sky and—to a certain extent—the ocean. The rest of the scene suffers from underexposure. This would be a challenge for Levels, but Curves copes with ease.

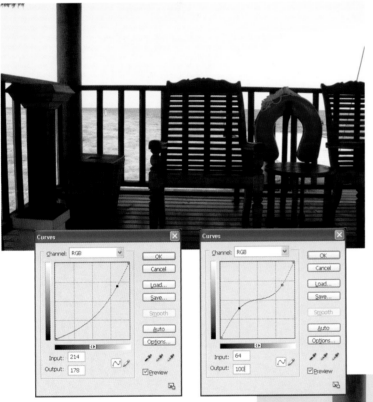

1 Press Ctrl/Cmd + M (**Image > Adjustments > Curves**). The brighter parts of the image are defined along the top half of the diagonal line. Click and drag the line from a point as shown in the example. (To replicate this sample curve exactly, type the numbers into the Input and Output boxes in the Curves dialog box—select the points on the curve to activate the boxes.) Dragging the diagonal line downwards darkens RGB images. Now the sky and ocean no longer look washed out. Don't click OK yet, though. This sweeping curve darkens the whole image, which isn't actually what we want. The lower half of the diagonal line represents the darker parts of the image, and as this line is now lower than the original position, the dark areas have become darker still.

2 Luckily, this isn't a problem, as Curves gives us the flexibility to edit up to 14 different points of brightness between white and black. Click and drag the curve from a point on the lower half of the line. Alternatively, just click to make a point on the line anywhere below the current existing point and type the numbers shown into the Input and Output boxes. The resulting image has enhanced contrast in the sky and ocean, while improving visibility in the darker areas.

16

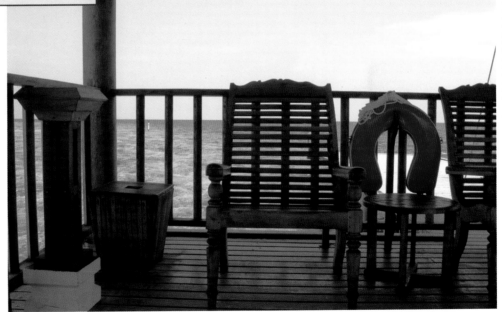

Users of Photoshop CS2 have a more powerful and intuitive exposure-correction tool within their grasp. Go to **Image** > **Adjustments** > **Exposure**.

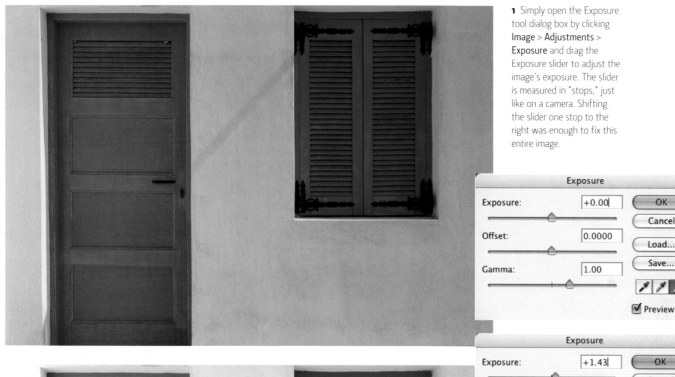

1 Simply open the Exposure tool dialog box by clicking **Image** > **Adjustments** > **Exposure** and drag the Exposure slider to adjust the image's exposure. The slider is measured in "stops," just like on a camera. Shifting the slider one stop to the right was enough to fix this entire image.

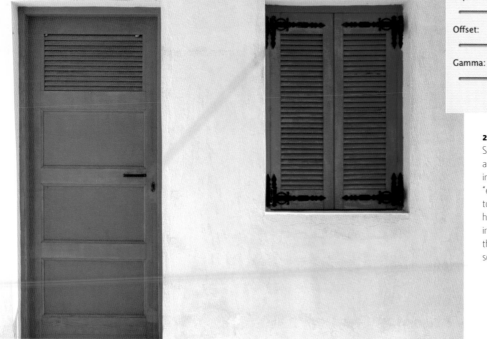

2 Alternatively, select the Set White Point eyedropper and click somewhere on the image's subject. The "exposure" will be adjusted to appear as if the object had been correctly metered in the first place. Either way, the result should look something like this.

Tip

If you've moved over to the RAW format on your digital camera, you can deal with many exposure problems within the Camera RAW plug-in. See page 140 for details.

17

Controlling contrast

The same controls used to adjust levels of brightness also come into play in correcting areas of weak or excessive contrast. In fact, poor contrast is usually a direct result of poor exposure. The two are so closely linked as to share a common tool—the Brightness/Contrast command—though, as we mentioned on the previous pages, this tool isn't particularly effective in real-world use. As with brightness, contrast is better adjusted using more sophisticated methods.

Method 1: **Automatic options**

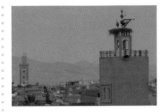

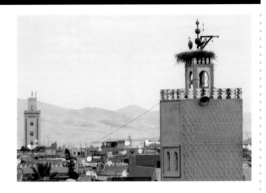

For a quick fix, try the automated Auto Levels and Auto Contrast commands. Both work well on some images, but Auto Levels can create new problems at the same time as it solves old ones.

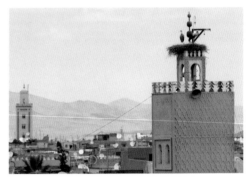

1 As Auto Levels works on each channel independently, it has a tendency to produce a color cast, and can fail to remove one when that would seem an obvious step to the human eye. Take this tonally flat landscape shot, for example. **Select Image > Adjustments > Auto Levels** (Cmd/Ctrl+Shift+L).

2 Now we'll compare the result of Auto Levels by doing the same thing with Auto Contrast. Work on another copy of the original, and select **Image > Adjustments > Auto Contrast** (Ctrl/Cmd + Alt + Shift + L). Both commands succeed in increasing contrast, but the Auto Levels version has a cyan cast creeping in.

Method 2: **Levels**

For greater control, the manual Levels command is a better choice. Here the sun-bleached stones leave this desert image looking dull, and the whole shot suffers from a lack of tonal contrast.

1 Select **Image > Adjustments > Levels** (Ctrl/Cmd + L). As we detailed on pages 14 to 15, moving the black slider to the right and the white slider to the left will help with over- and underexposure, but the closer the black and white sliders come together, the greater the contrast will be. It's wise to judge the effect by eye, enabling the Preview checkbox to assess just how close they should be. The gray or gamma slider in the middle can also be employed: drag it right to darken the midtones and

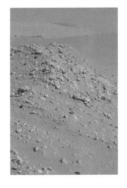

left to lighten them. This simple Levels adjustment transforms the picture, giving it a much greater visual impact.

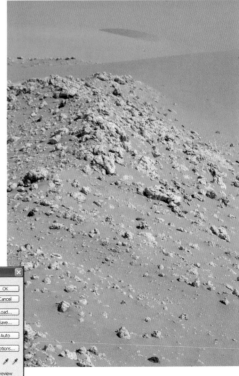

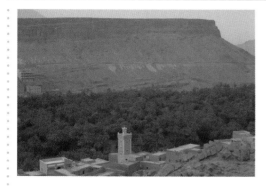

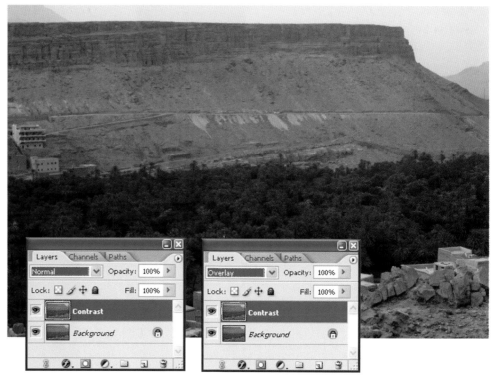

This is a slightly more unorthodox method for correcting contrast, but it's quick and often effective.

1 Take this hazy shot, and duplicate the background layer, either by dragging it to the New Layer icon at the bottom of the Layers palette, or by selecting **Layer** > **New** > **Duplicate Layer**.

2 Now change the duplicate layer's blend mode to Overlay. The new image has increased contrast, and a richer overall look.

Tip

CURVES

We can get exactly the same effect using the Curves command. Select Image > Adjustment > Curves (Ctrl/Cmd + M)—but this time we won't actually make a curve. Instead, bring the white and black points closer together to ramp up the contrast. First click and drag the white point at the top right corner of the diagonal line slightly down to the left, then drag the black point in the bottom left corner of the line to the right. Try experimenting with the proximity of the black and white points to each other to see different degrees of contrast.

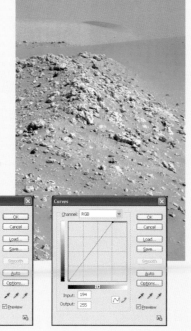

SOFT LIGHT

For something more subtle, try the Soft Light blend mode instead. The results with different blend modes will differ from image to image, depending on their tone and color characteristics, so it's well worth experimenting.

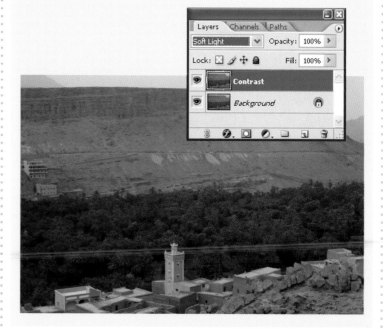

Difficult exposure problems

The methods we've already covered are the bread and butter of Photoshop corrections, and highly successful in most cases. However, every photo shoot produces some images that present additional problems, requiring extra work.

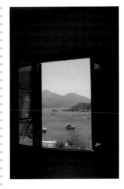

The scene through the open window presents one of the most common exposure problems. The photograph was exposed for the outside, and this has rendered the interior very dark. We could use any of the techniques we've already covered, but in this case a different approach—treating the photo as if it were two separate images—will give us a much better result.

1 Make a selection of the exterior view through the window using the Polygonal Lasso. Now invert that selection by going to **Select** > **Inverse** (Ctrl/Cmd + Shift + I).

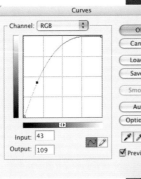

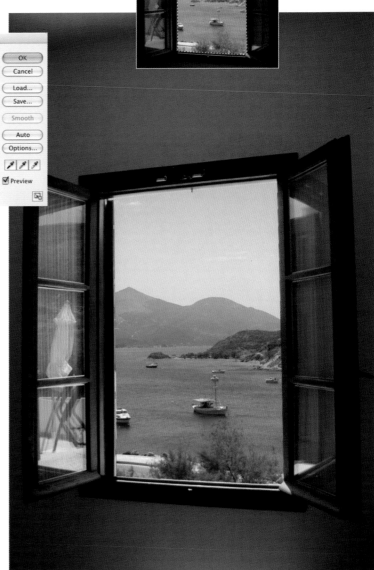

2 Choose **Image** > **Adjustments** > **Curves** (Ctrl/Cmd + M) to open the Curves palette. Reproduce the curve in the example to lighten the selection. The protected exterior view remains unchanged, revealing a better overall balance in the image.

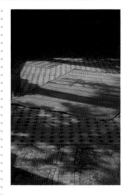

Although it's difficult to tell, this image should contain a lot of detail in the shadows. Sadly, exposing for the bright patches of sunlight has caused the shadows to look essentially black. The extremes of the heavy black shadow and the bright sunlight proved too much for the camera, but we can still keep the dappled sunlight—which is very flattering on the mosaic floor and rugs—while lightening up the shadows. Photoshop CS can handle this difficult task with ease. Go to **Image** > **Adjustments** > **Shadow/Highlight**.

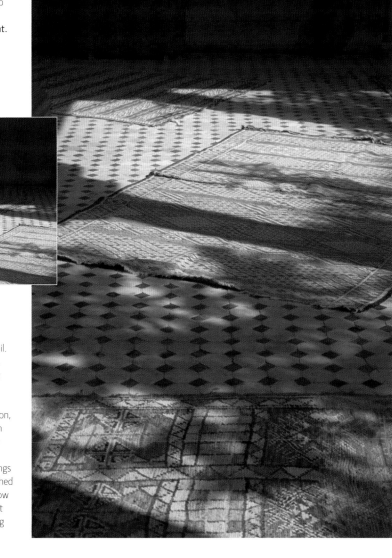

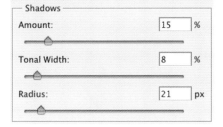

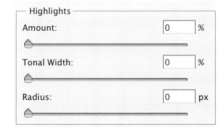

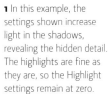

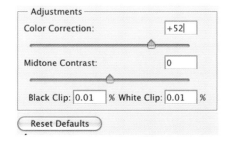

1 In this example, the settings shown increase light in the shadows, revealing the hidden detail. The highlights are fine as they are, so the Highlight settings remain at zero.

2 In the adjustment section, Color Correction has been boosted to +52, with the Midtone Contrast, Black Clip, and White Clip settings left unchanged. The finished image has stronger shadow detail, but the adjustment hasn't affected the strong play of sunlight.

21

Difficult exposure problems

The Shadow/Highlight tool excels in situations where shadows need darkening but other areas are generally well exposed. It's far more than a dumb brightness adjustment tool, as it makes adjustments based on surrounding pixels in the shadows and highlight areas. This enables us to make independent adjustments to the shadows or the highlights, without the usual adverse effects.

When the dialog box opens, the options are set by default to correct problems of backlighting. If that isn't your immediate problem, you can adjust the controls manually. Click the Show More Options checkbox to reveal the full range of settings.

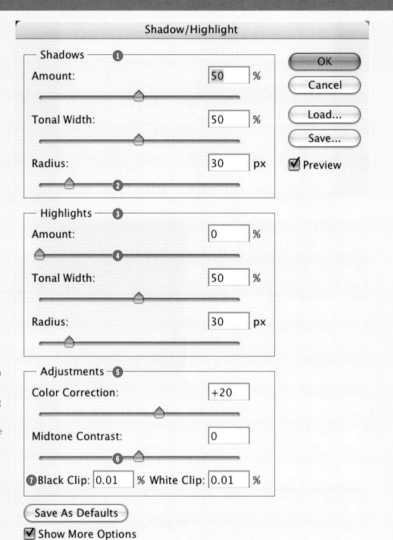

1 SHADOWS

The Tonal Width slider is used to specify how many tones are modified in the shadows. A low setting will affect only the darkest areas of the shadows, leaving other areas untouched. As the value is increased the midtones of the shadows are also modified. With higher values comes a risk of halos appearing where there are strong light to dark edges. Keep the preview checkbox enabled to monitor this.

2 RADIUS

The Radius slider defines the size of the pixel area surrounding a given pixel that is used to assess whether it fits in the shadows or the highlights. Higher values result in larger areas. The setting will vary depending on the size of the image and the size of the area you're adjusting. Too low, and it might not affect the whole target area. Too high, and it might affect areas you don't want changed. If Shadow/Highlight doesn't seem to be working, set the Amount to maximum (so you can see the effect) and nudge the Radius steadily left or right. When the filter seems to be affecting only the parts you want adjusted, stop and return to the Amount setting to continue the adjustment.

3 AMOUNT

The Amount slider governs the percentage amount of adjustment based on the tonal width and radius settings. Higher values result in increased lightening of the shadows, but overdoing it causes a problematic loss of contrast in the shadow areas.

4 HIGHLIGHTS

The same controls exist for highlights. In this case increasing the Amount slider will darken the highlights and Lower Tonal Width settings will affect only the brightest areas of the highlights. The Radius controls work the same way as the Shadows controls.

5 ADJUSTMENTS

Use the Color Correction slider to make any color adjustments to any areas revealed by your Shadow or Highlight adjustments: the adjustments made will only apply to pixels affected by your corrections so far. Moving the slider right saturates the pixels, while moving the slider left tones them down.

6 MIDTONE CONTRAST

Midtone Contrast can be increased by dragging the Midtone contrast slider to the right, or reduced by dragging it to the left. A shift to the right may also make shadows darker and highlights brighter.

7 BLACK CLIP & WHITE CLIP

Use the Black Clip and White Clip values to determine the extent to which the shadows and highlights will be clipped to the new shadow and highlight settings. Shadow is 0 and highlight is 255. Larger values boost the contrast in the image but can also reduce detail, as the extreme values will be clipped to black or white.

Other images demand a more specific approach, where areas of an image are adjusted manually using two tools with their origins in the traditional darkroom. The Dodge and Burn tools are highly effective at lightening and darkening small regions of an image, or emphasizing the effects of light and shadow.

The Burn Tool

The patterned glass image has a couple of highlight areas that are nearly completely blown-out. Using the Burn tool, we can darken these areas and regain some of the detail.

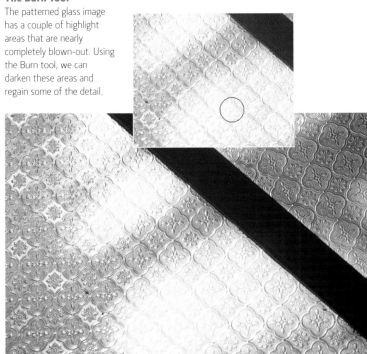

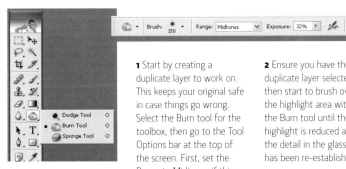

1 Start by creating a duplicate layer to work on. This keeps your original safe in case things go wrong. Select the Burn tool for the toolbox, then go to the Tool Options bar at the top of the screen. First, set the Range to Midtones if this option hasn't already been chosen by default. It may seem more logical to select Highlights, but this would actually cause an excessively harsh result. Set the Exposure to 31% to create subtle, realistic results.

2 Ensure you have the duplicate layer selected, then start to brush over the highlight area with the Burn tool until the highlight is reduced and the detail in the glass has been re-established.

The Dodge Tool

While the Burn tool makes short work of overblown highlights and localized overexposure, the Dodge tool is perfect for manual retouching of areas where too much shadow is the problem. In this example, we'll use it to lighten some of the craftwork above the terrace window.

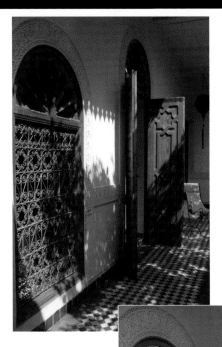

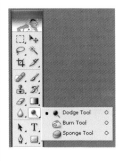

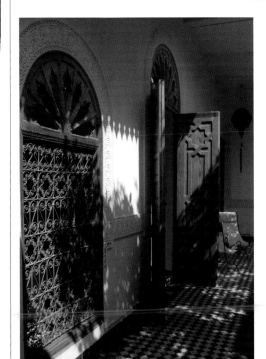

1 Once again, work on a duplicate layer. Select the Dodge tool, with the Range set to Midtones and the Exposure set to below 50% for the most subtle effect. Work carefully to lighten the craftwork above the door.

2 The selected details have been emphasized without affecting the overall atmosphere of the image, or its high-contrast play of light and shadow.

23

COLOR CORRECTION

Strengthening color

Saturating color

Working with color casts

Strengthening color

Correcting exposure will solve many basic color problems, but Photoshop's extensive range of color correction tools can easily handle any that are left over. For example, overexposure or poor lighting conditions can give a photograph a distinctly washed-out look, which may persist when the initial fault is fixed. Photoshop offers several ways of boosting color. We'll explore three of them in our attempts to enhance this lackluster shot.

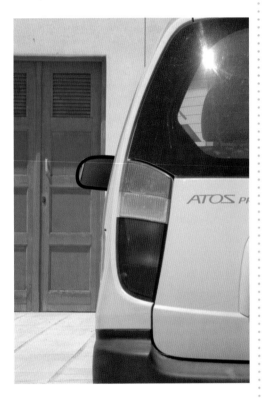

Method 1: **Hue/Saturation**

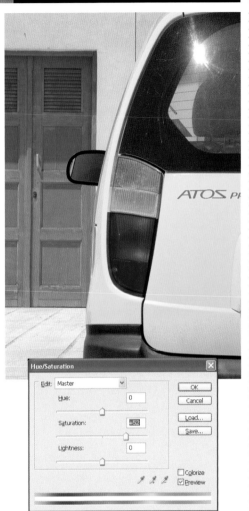

The first tool, the Hue/Saturation dialog box, is one of the easiest and most intuitive to use. Boosting the Saturation has an instant strengthening effect on all the colors in an image.

1 Select Image > Adjustments > Hue/Saturation (Ctrl/Cmd + U). The adjustment is a simple one. We want to keep the original colors in the scene, but with an increased level of intensity. Drag the Saturation slider to the right. With the preview check box enabled you can judge the degree of adjustment needed by eye. Click OK, and this rather nondescript image becomes a bold color statement.

Alternatively, you can select specific colors from the drop-down box and adjust those individually.

Method 2: **Curves**

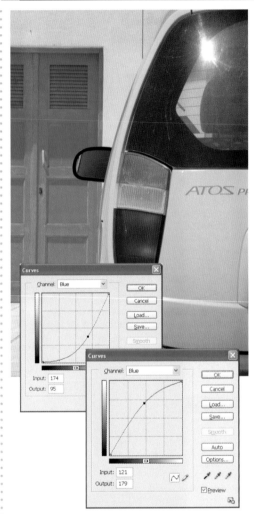

The same principles apply to both the Curves and Levels commands. Adjusting the individual color channels enables you to boost certain colors at the expense of others.

1 Open the original image and select the car (as in step 1 of method 3). Go to Image > Adjustments > Curves (Ctrl/Cmd + M). Select Blue from the Channel drop-down. Click in the centre of the diagonal line and drag that point down to decrease the strength of blue and create a more vibrant yellow.

2 Now select the blue doors and relaunch the Curves dialog box. Return to the Blue channel, and select a central point, then drag it upwards. This mirrors the Curve in the last step, and has the opposite effect: strengthening the blues and reducing the yellows. The effect is similar to the result achieved with Levels.

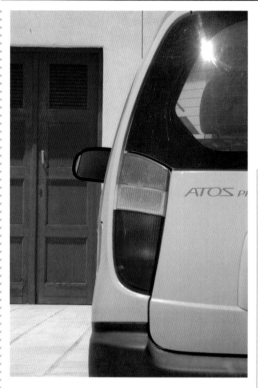

The Levels command is closely associated with brightness and contrast adjustments, but it's also a powerful color control. Adjustments made to the levels of individual color channels affect specific colors, and can be used to boost them or control the overall balance. Think of each RGB channel in terms of a range running between a pair of complementary colors. In the Red channel, we can interpret the white marker as red and the black marker as cyan. Similarly the Green channel translates white as magenta and black as green, and the Blue channel runs from yellow to blue.

1 We can put the theory into practice. First make a selection of the yellow portions of the car. The easiest way to do this is using the Color Range selection tool. Set the Fuzziness to 50 and make an initial selection, then use the + Eyedropper to add to it. The selection doesn't need to be perfectly accurate as long as it contains most of the car and none of the background.

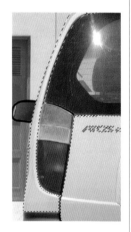

2 Now go to **Image > Adjustments > Levels** (Ctrl/Cmd + L). To edit the yellow portions, select the Blue channel from the Channel drop-down menu (yellow and blue are opposites). Dragging the black marker (which we can interpret as yellow) to the right will emphasize and strengthen the yellow in the selection, while diminishing any blues. The amount you drag depends on the intensity of the color you desire. The extreme adjustment shown here results in a rich, bold yellow.

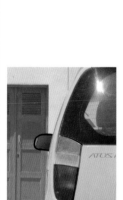

3 Next, make a selection of the blue doors. Launch the Levels dialog box and select the Blue channel again. This time, drag the white marker (think of it as blue) to the left to increase the blue component in the selection and reduce the yellow. This creates a strong saturated blue for the doors.

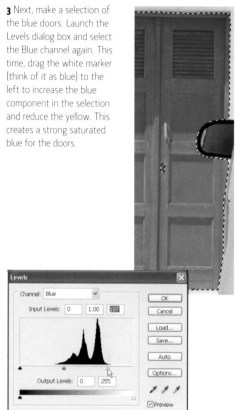

4 We can fine-tune colors by making further adjustments to other channels on the same selection. To make the blue doors closer to a royal blue, for instance, edit the green channel and move the black marker (think of it as magenta) to the right. This diminishes the green, and results in a rich blue, infused with purple.

27

PHOTOSHOP COLOR THEORY

Adjusting colors in Photoshop requires a small amount of color theory. Look at the color wheel below. The colors that sit opposite each other are called complementary colors. Red is opposite to cyan, green is opposite to magenta, and blue is opposite to yellow. In many Photoshop dialog boxes—Levels, Curves, or Color Balance for example—strengthening or diminishing one color will have the opposite effect on its complement. We'll use this effect in methods 2 and 3 on this page, and in future projects throughout the book.

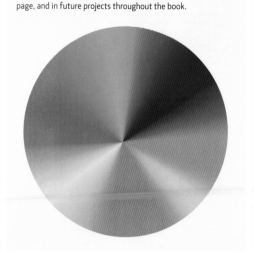

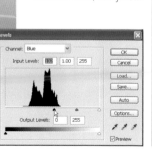

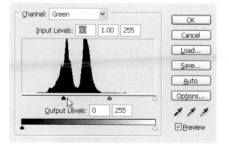

Saturating color

Another method of boosting color is to use the Selective Color command. This technique offers one key advantage: it doesn't require any selections to be made. This shot of a Mediterranean fishing village has a liberal scattering of boldly painted woodwork, but the exposure has failed to capture the vibrancy of the original scene.

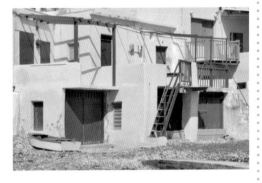

Using selective color

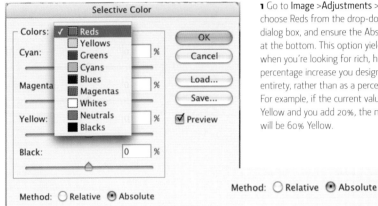

Method: ◯ Relative ⦿ Absolute

1 Go to Image >Adjustments > Selective Color. First, choose Reds from the drop-down box at the top of the dialog box, and ensure the Absolute radio button is enabled at the bottom. This option yields a more pronounced effect when you're looking for rich, heavily saturated color. The percentage increase you designate will be applied in its entirety, rather than as a percentage of the original number. For example, if the current value of a certain pixel is 40% Yellow and you add 20%, the new total value of that pixel will be 60% Yellow.

2 To enrich the reds, first reduce the percentage of the Cyan. This shifts the selected color towards the warmer red end of the color spectrum. Increases in percentage to the magenta and yellow will amplify this effect. To assess the color change, enable the Preview checkbox.

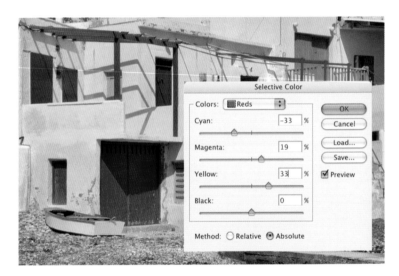

3 Now for the blues. Select Blues from the same drop-down menu. For a rich Mediterranean blue, increase the Cyan and Magenta percentages and reduce the Yellow percentage.

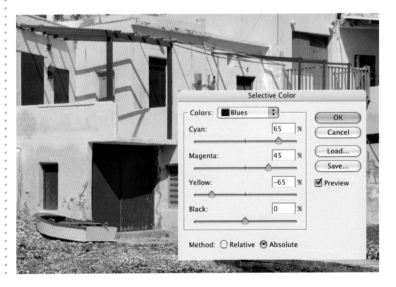

28

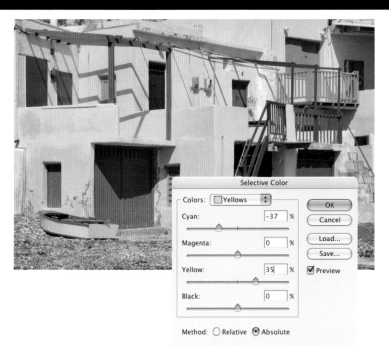

4 The orange woodwork is next. Choose Yellow from the drop-down box and reduce the Cyan proportion while increasing the Yellow. You may want to experiment with the Magenta at this point. Increasing the percentage will show a bias towards the red end of the color spectrum, resulting in richer, red oranges. Decreasing the percentage leans towards the yellow end for a paler orange. Alternatively, leave the Magenta at 0% for an orange somewhere between these two extremes.

5 Finally the aqua-colored woodwork needs some adjustment to distinguish it from the blues. Select the Cyans from the drop-down box. Increase the percentage of Cyan and Yellow and reduce the Magenta. Greater percentages of Yellow create a strong, oceanic turquoise. The finished result is resplendent in its glorious hues—just the way it was meant to be.

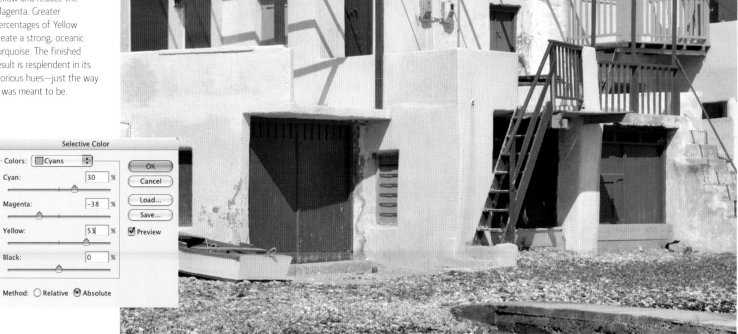

Working with color casts

A color cast describes an overwhelming predominance of a certain color throughout an image—as if the shot had been taken through a tinted filter, shifting the hue of every color in the scene. Color casts are easy enough to correct, but we need to be sure of the nature of the cast in order to make the right adjustment. Some are unmistakable, while others need a more experienced eye to discern between, say, a yellow or green cast. Luckily, Photoshop offers an alternative while you develop that expertise.

RECOGNIZING COLOR CASTS

Study the picture of the white flowers carefully. You may be able to recognize a yellow cast permeating the entire image.

To confirm the nature of the color cast, make sure the info palette is open (Window > Info) then select the Eyedropper tool from the toolbox. Keep the mouse button pressed while hovering over a pale part of the flower petal. We would expect this area to have a neutral color, where the RGB values are virtually equal. For instance white should be R255, G255, B255, and this would be consistent all the way through the range of grays down to black (R0, G0, B0). In this image, however, the RGB section of the Info palette confirms that the pixel has more red and green than blue. In RGB color, red and green make yellow, so we now have conclusive proof of a yellow color cast.

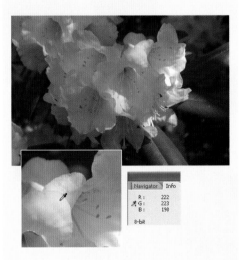

Method 1: **Variations**

The Variations command is an easy, visual method, best suited to photographs that don't require detailed fine-tuning. Go to **Image** > **Adjustments** > **Variations**.

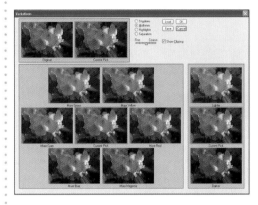

2 The next image shows the result of an additional click on More Blue (the effects are cumulative).

1 The two thumbnails in the top left of the dialog box show the original and adjusted versions of the image. These should be identical when the dialog box opens, but if you have used Variations recently, the adjusted thumbnail will display the current image with the Variations setting you used. Click on the Original thumbnail to reset it. The thumbnails below show the approximate result of choosing that variation. These give you an "at a glance" idea of what variation is needed to fix the current color problem. We know this image has a bias of red and green resulting in a yellow cast. Logically, adding more blue would compensate, so click More Blue.

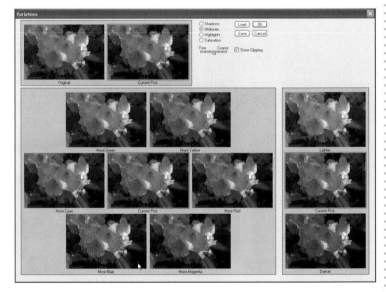

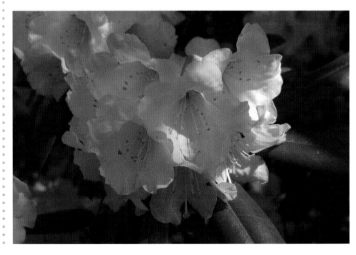

The Levels command offers a powerful tool for color cast removal. Keeping in mind the neutral color principle, we can use Levels to do most of the thinking for us. The overall pink tint of our next image is a sure sign of a magenta color cast.

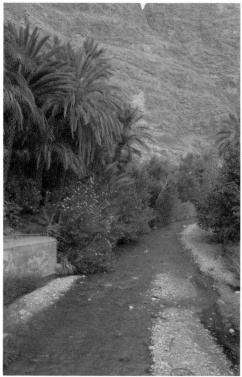

1 Go to **Window > Info** to open the Info palette, then press Ctrl/Cmd + L to bring up Levels. Before we fix the color cast, we need to set the white and black points for the image. Examine the shot carefully, and look for elements of the image that should be pure white or pure black. Select the Black eyedropper above the Preview box, then use the Info palette to find the darkest area of the image (the RGB values should be as close to 0 as possible). When you've narrowed your search down to a specific region, zoom in so you can see the individual pixels. Click on the darkest pixel to set the Black point. Then select the White eyedropper, and repeat the process, looking for the lightest area of the image (in this case, the RGB values on the Info palette should be as close to 255 as possible).

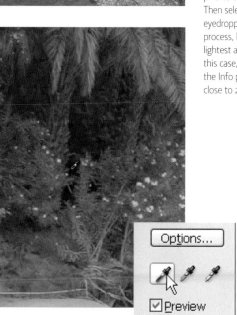

The quickest way to remove a color cast requires no input or expertise whatsoever. Go to Image > Adjustments > Auto Color. It's quick and easy, but for the best results it's wise to use a method that gives you more control.

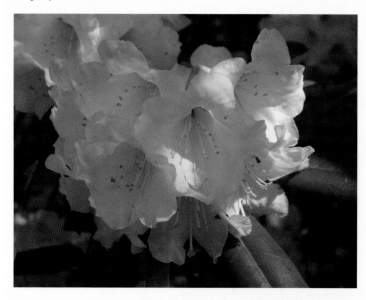

2 Now choose the gamma (gray) Eyedropper. Look for a part of the image that would be a neutral gray. In this case one of the stones in the river will serve the purpose well. Click the chosen part of the image with the gamma eyedropper. The magenta cast has now been removed.

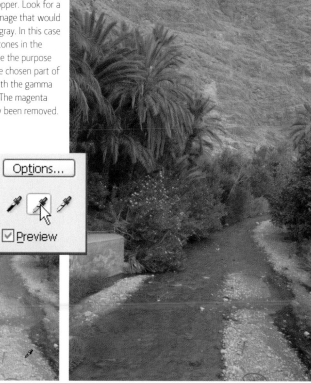

Dealing with color casts

Method 3: **Channel adjustments**

If further adjustment is needed we can delve deeper into Levels. The real power of the tool is in its individual channel operations. Reload the original image, select **Image > Adjustments > Levels**, and click on the Green channel in the Channels drop-down.

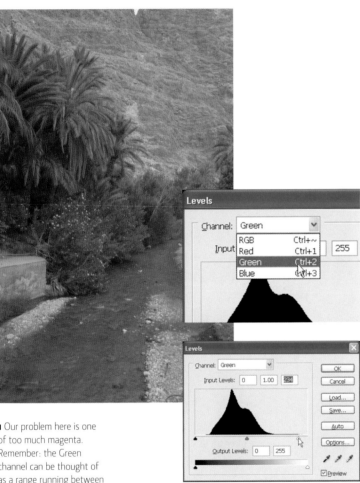

1 Our problem here is one of too much magenta. Remember: the Green channel can be thought of as a range running between the green and magenta, with Green the right slider (white) and Magenta the left (black). To make a magenta reduction, drag the white slider to the left to a value of about 234. The benefit of this method is that you can decide exactly how much magenta to remove. To make it obvious, in this example I chose a value that goes too far. You can now see a slight green cast creeping in when you compare this image with the previous correction.

Method 4: **Color balance**

The Color Balance command is one of the easiest to understand. Press Ctrl/Cmd + B (**Image > Adjustments > Color Balance**). We can see the complementary colors neatly laid out, and as long as we know which colors we want corrected, we can drag the appropriate slider.

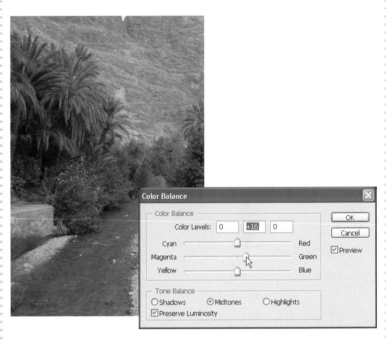

1 Drag the Magenta/Green slider towards the green. This reduces the magenta and will eventually increase the green if you drag far enough. With the Midtones radio button selected, the adjustment will be restricted to the midtones of the image, with less impact on the shadows and highlights.

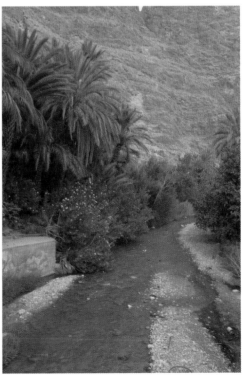

The final method uses Curves—the more experienced you become with Photoshop, the more you'll realize how useful this multi-faceted tool can be.

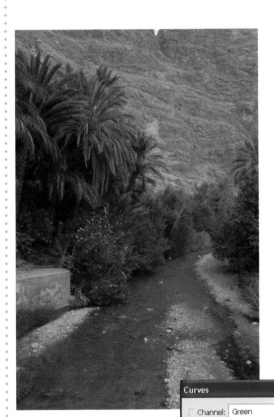

1 Select **Image > Adjustments > Curves** (Ctrl/Cmd + M). We are still using the principle of complementary colors here, so choose the Green channel from the Channel drop-down. Move the pointer to the centre of the diagonal line, and drag upwards to reduce the magenta in the midtones. The more you drag, the more you will reduce the magenta and increase green, with the effect spreading to the highlights and shadows. As the finished image shows, even minor adjustments can change the appearance of a photograph quite radically.

TIP

Of course, not all color casts are bad, and there are times when removing one does your image a disservice. In this case, an early morning Alpine shot, it's the blue light reflecting from the snow that makes the image so atmospheric. With the blue cast removed, the whole image looks wrong.

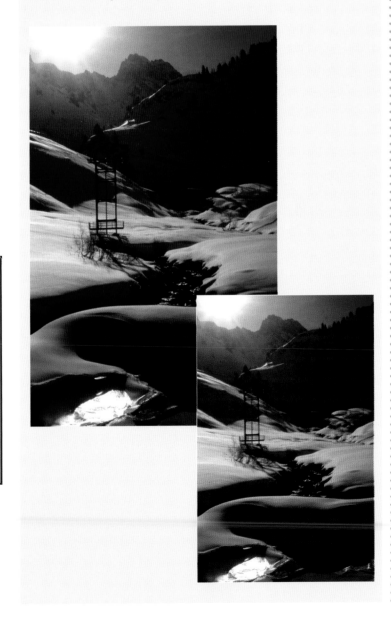

33

FOCUS MANIPULATION

Sharpening images

Soft focus techniques

Depth of field effects

Motion blurring

Sharpening images

After color and brightness corrections, image sharpening is probably the most-used function in Photoshop. Although there's no substitute for shooting the original photograph in focus, Photoshop's sharpening tools can greatly improve the quality of less-than-optimal originals. These tools don't actually improve the focus—instead, they increase the contrast along edges where different tonal areas meet, which creates the illusion of a sharper image.

Method 1: **Smart Sharpen**

While Photoshop has four different sharpening filters, Sharpen, Sharpen Edges and Sharpen More are really best saved for "quick and dirty" fixes. For many years, the Unsharp Mask has been the professional's choice, as it offers more control. However, Photoshop CS2 introduces the Smart Sharpen filter, which has been designed to remove the effects of camera shake or slightly inaccurate focusing. It doesn't replace the Unsharp Mask, but it can be easier and more effective provided you can identify the basic problem.

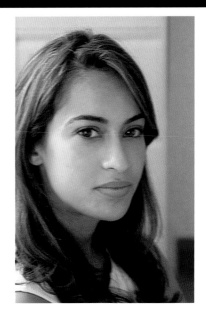

1 Open the image and take a careful look. Is it slightly out of focus (Lens blur)? Has it been blurred during image editing or is it, as in this case, the victim of some camera shake? Either way, click **Filter > Sharpen > Smart Sharpen**.

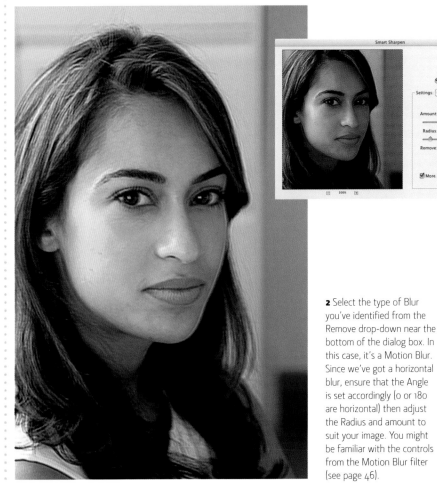

2 Select the type of Blur you've identified from the Remove drop-down near the bottom of the dialog box. In this case, it's a Motion Blur. Since we've got a horizontal blur, ensure that the Angle is set accordingly (0 or 180 are horizontal) then adjust the Radius and amount to suit your image. You might be familiar with the controls from the Motion Blur filter (see page 46).

Users of Photoshop CS and older versions will have to stick to the tried and trusted Unsharp Mask (**Filter** > **Sharpen** > **Unsharp Mask**). We'll use it here on a poorly focused shot.

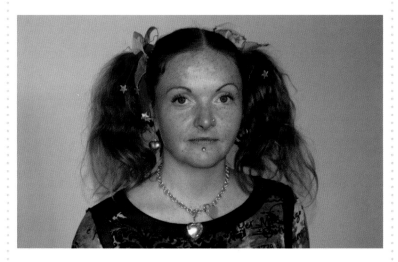

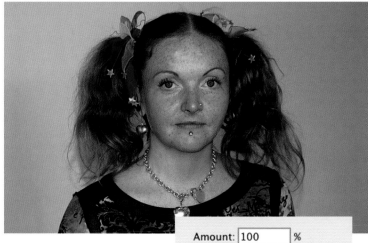

1 In this example, set the Amount to 100%, the Radius to 1.5 and the Threshold to 0. The result is a crisper image, and it would be quite acceptable to leave it there. However, as we are dealing with a portrait, we may not want such a sharp image—at least not across the whole photo. Although the filter has sharpened the area around the eyes, it has also sharpened the skin texture, along with imperfections that were previously concealed by the soft focus.

The Unsharp Mask provides a dialog box and settings that enable a controlled approach to sharpening. By adjusting the three sliders and checking the results in the Preview window, we can ensure that our sharpening goes far enough to be effective, but not so far as to ruin the image.

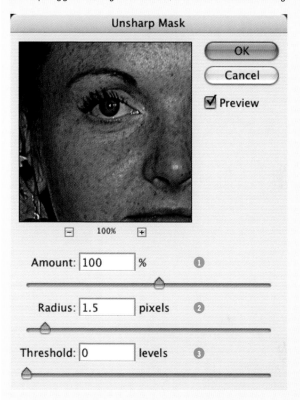

① AMOUNT

This dictates how much sharpening is applied. Although it's tempting to apply high values to some images, the results won't be kind to your subject. Use the Preview window to judge the point at which sharpening becomes unacceptable.

② RADIUS

The Unsharp Mask works by finding edges in the image, then increasing the contrast on those edges. The Radius setting refers to how thick these edges should be, with higher settings resulting in thicker edges. The resolution of the file is the most important factor in determining what radius to use. Higher resolutions need higher settings, but—as with the Amount—a higher setting can have a negative impact on the image. Again, use the Preview to avoid going too far.

③ THRESHOLD

This setting defines what Photoshop considers an edge, and what it ignores, in terms of how different the brightness values have to be between neighboring pixels before those pixels will be sharpened. The range runs from 0 to 255, where lower values permit a greater part of the image to be sharpened, while higher values limit the sharpening to areas of high contrast.

37

Sharpening images

Method 3: **Sharpening with masks**

One way of gaining even more control over the Unsharp Mask is to make a mask of the critical areas beforehand. Don't worry if you're not a master of manual selections: we have a useful shortcut we can follow.

1 Open another copy of the original image and open the Channels palette. Now find a channel with good contrast, so that the eyes and lips stand out from the rest of the image. In this example, the Green channel fits the bill perfectly, but this wouldn't be the case with every shot—if the image was predominantly green, the Red or Blue channels might give you better results.

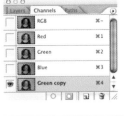

2 Copy the Green channel, as we'll use this as the foundation for our mask (since we are working on a copy, our changes won't have any impact on the original colors). First, go to **Filter > Stylize > Find Edges**. This gives us a good automated starting point. Now invert the image using **Image > Adjust > Invert** (or Ctrl/Cmd + I).

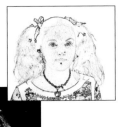

3 The main areas that need sharpening stand out, but we can make them even more obvious using Levels (Ctrl/Cmd + L). By generating some extreme contrast, we can ensure that most of the face texture is blacked out, leaving the eyes, mouth, and the edges of the hair, jewelry, and clothing white. We want a histogram that leans strongly towards the darker end, so move the Shadows slider in.

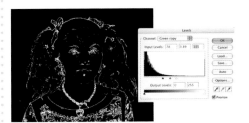

4 Although we can now see the areas that will be sharpened, any hard black-to-white transitions will make the Sharpen filter look false when applied. To remedy this go to **Filter > Blur > Gaussian Blur**.

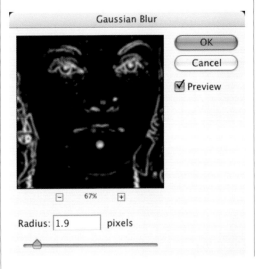

Set the Radius to 1.9 and click OK. This has a feathering effect on the hard edges and, once the mask is in place, will ensure the final sharpening effect is applied with more subtlety than before.

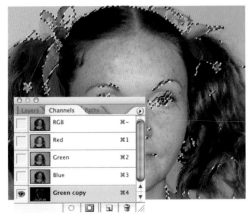

5 With the mask finished, we can load it as a selection. To do so, press and hold the Ctrl/Cmd key, then click the Green copy channel in the Channels palette. Now activate the RGB composite channel, then return to the Layers palette. Make sure you can see the marching ants of the loaded selection.

6 Apply the Unsharp Mask filter as before, using the same settings to make a direct comparison. You should see a subtle difference between the two, with a softer skin texture that contrasts with the well-defined eyes, mouth, and jewelry, or the sharp detail in the clothing and accessories. If the image doesn't seem sharp enough, you may want to lower the Radius setting.

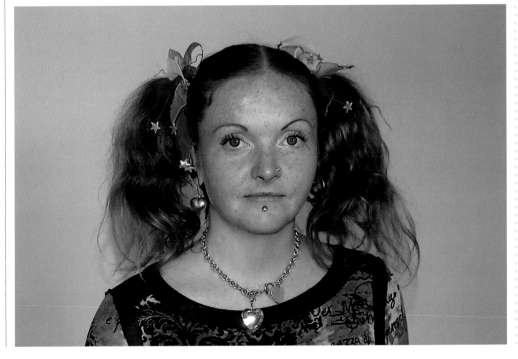

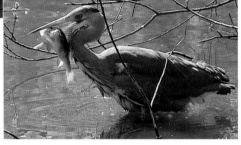

In some cases, a more localized form of sharpening is required. For example, I was in such a rush to capture this rare image of a heron having just caught an oversized fish that I didn't have time to focus. As a result, the image is a little soft—particularly in the bird's eye and in some of the detail of the fish. The Unsharp Mask filter would help, but it also sharpens a lot of incidental noise, giving the image a grainy feel.

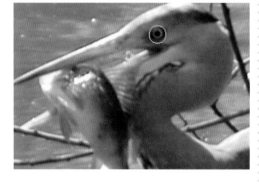

1 For these small areas of isolated sharpening, the manual Sharpen tool is as quick and flexible to use as a paintbrush. It shares the same location as the Blur and Smudge tools in the toolbox (click and hold on the Blur or Smudge to see the alternative tools flyout if the Sharpen tool isn't currently visible). As we paint in the sharpening effect, we can ignore the feathers and the water, and concentrate on the areas in need of sharpening. For control over areas of fine detail, set the size of the brush and the strength of the sharpening in the Tool Options bar at the top of the screen, or use the square bracket keys ([and]) to increase and decrease the brush size.

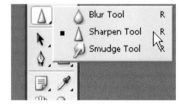

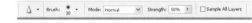

2 With the size set to 30 and the strength set to 50%, click to apply sharpening to the bird's eye and the scales of the fish as needed. The same caveats apply as when using the sharpen filters—oversharpening results in an unsightly "pixelation" effect, which becomes more obvious as you keep sharpening.

3 In photographs where eyes appear, they often become the focal point of the image. By sharpening them selectively, as here, we can create the feel of a crisper image, without degrading elements of the image that are better left soft.

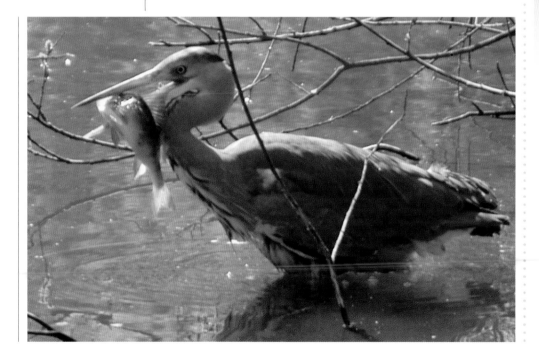

39

Soft focus techniques

Despite photography's obsession with clarity and capturing detail, sharp focus isn't the be-all and end-all. In some situations, the opposite is desirable. In some female portrait styles, including the classic Hollywood studio publicity shot, a deliberate soft focus effect is used to evoke a sense of romance, or to create a dreamy, ethereal world. In traditional photography, the methods employed to achieve this range from dedicated soft focus filters, to gauze over the lens, to smearing a diffusing gel over a piece of glass on the front of the lens. Photoshop's methods are equally varied, but offer a greater degree of control.

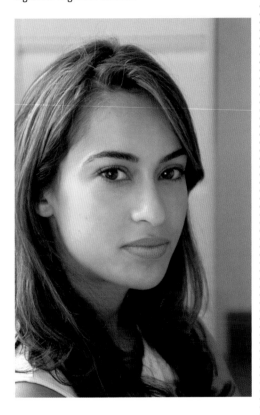

Method 1: **Gaussian Blur**

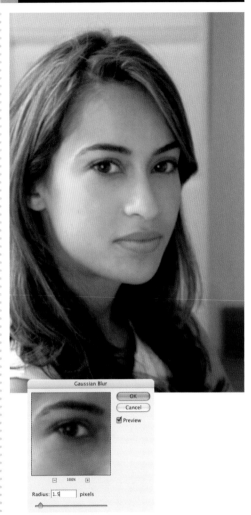

The quickest technique is to use the versatile Gaussian Blur filter. This helps to cancel out any lines, blemishes or harsh lighting.

1 Select **Filter > Blur > Gaussian Blur**. The Radius applied will depend upon the resolution of the image—for higher resolutions, higher Radius settings will be required to achieve the same effect as a low setting on a low-resolution image. A fine line divides a setting that softens an image and a setting that merely looks out of focus, but that line is quite subjective. The effect here is subtle, but the method has one key drawback: critical areas such as the eyes and lips lose their impact as a result of the softening. One way around this is to mask those areas prior to blurring, but there are easier and more effective techniques.

Method 2: **Gaussian Blur (advanced)**

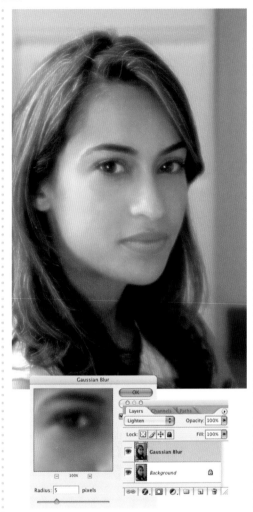

For a more highly finished, sophisticated effect we can use the Gaussian Blur filter in combination with a change of blend mode.

1 Starting with the original image, create a duplicate layer and apply a Gaussian Blur with a Radius of 5.0. In itself, this setting is far too high and blurs the image out of recognition.

2 Change the blurred layer's blending mode to Lighten, and the result is reminiscent of that old Hollywood publicity shot, where the skin tones are softened and a gentle light pervades the whole scene. With this method the eyes and lips maintain their impact without the need for any additional selections.

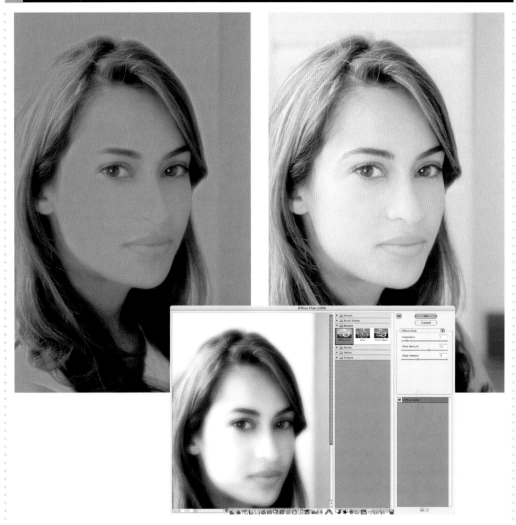

If you want a slightly stronger effect, use the Median filter with another blend mode, Screen.

1 Go back to the original image, create a duplicate layer, and apply the Median filter (**Filter > Noise > Median**) with the Radius set to 1.

2 Once again the effect on its own is too strong, but change the layer blend mode to Screen and reduce the opacity to 80%. The result is similar to the effect of Method 2, but with a greater spread of light and a reduction in skin texture and detail.

An alternative filter, Diffuse Glow, creates an even more pronounced effect, minimizing rough textures and further softening the edges of the eyes and lips.

1 Return to the original image and create a new duplicate layer. Set the background color to white, then select **Filter > Distort > Diffuse Glow**. Set the Graininess to 1, the Glow Amount to 12, and the Clear Amount to 7. The eyes and lips are still recognizable, but the overall look is significantly softer.

2 For a more detailed, less washed-out look, try reducing the layer's opacity—to 90% for the purposes of this example—and changing the blend mode to Screen.

41

Depth of field effects

There are other cases in which photographers may eschew pin-sharp focus in favor of a blurred effect, at least over part of the image. Using focus to isolate your subject from the background is a tried and trusted photographic technique, with the subject in sharp focus and the background blurred. In the camera, this is achieved through controlling the depth of field—the range in front of the lens where objects will remain in focus. Photoshop offers a range of techniques to reproduce the effect.

Method 1: **Selective blur**

The first technique is the simplest to apply, and works best if the subject is isolated on a single plane with all other elements of the image grouped closely together on another. The man in the straw hat makes a perfect projection screen for the light and shadow latticework falling from above, but the confusing background spoils the impact.

1 Make a selection of the subject using the Polygonal Lasso or the Extract command (see page 162). Invert the selection by pressing Ctrl/Cmd + I.

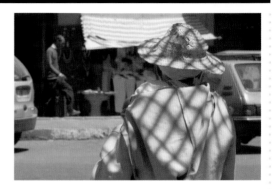

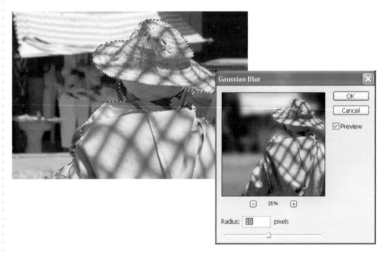

2 Now go to **Filter > Blur > Gaussian Blur**. The setting you apply depends on the degree of blurring desired, as well as the resolution of the working image. Higher resolutions need higher settings. Here, a Radius setting of 19 reduces the background to a muted color haze, effectively separating the subject from the confusion behind.

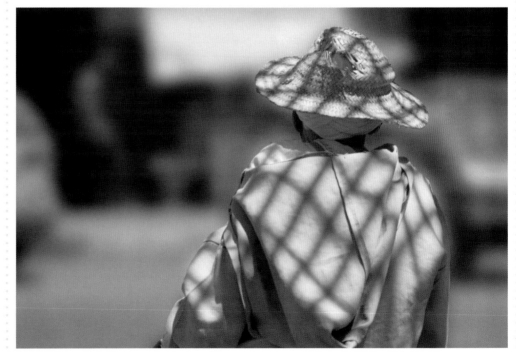

42

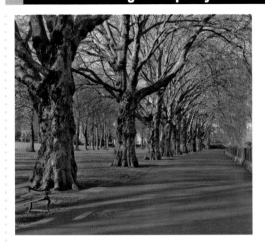

The previous method worked well with the image used, but its limitations soon become apparent if we try it with our next image. For a realistic effect, the degree of blurring should gradually increase or decrease to reflect the position of the objects within the frame and the depth of field you wish to simulate.

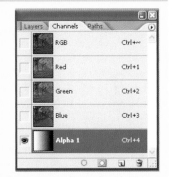

1 One way to achieve this is to use an opacity mask. First, go to the Channels palette and create a new channel, called "Blur Alpha." Now, with the new channel active, select the Gradient tool and drag a black-to-white linear gradient through the document from left to right. Hold down the Shift key as you drag to keep the gradient straight on the horizontal plane. We can define which areas are focussed or blurred—as well as how gradual the transition is between them—by fine tuning the linear gradient. The sharper the contrast of the gradient, the more abrupt the transition will be.

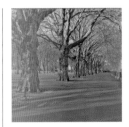

2 Click on the RGB Composite channel, then load the channel as a selection by pressing Ctrl/Cmd and clicking the Blur Alpha channel. (Alternatively you can load it as a selection by going to **Select > Load Selection** and choosing Blur Alpha from the drop-down box.) The selection's marquee outline doesn't show the true effect in terms of the selected area, but the gradient defines a gradual selection that goes from transparent, through semi-transparent, to opaque. The next image shows the selection loaded in Quick Mask mode. The semi-transparent area is more apparent, as the red of the quick mask gradually fades away.

3 Return to standard mode and apply the Gaussian blur filter to achieve a realistic narrow depth of field effect, just as the camera would capture it.

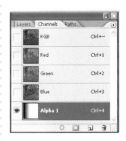

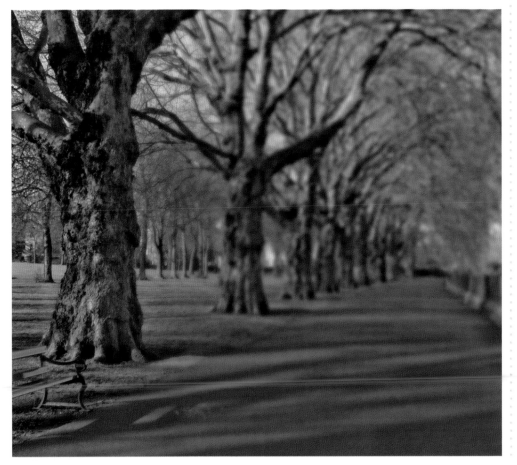

43

Depth of field effects

FOCUS MANIPULATION

Method 3: **Lens Blur**

Photoshop CS introduced a new method of handling depth of field: the Lens Blur filter. By using Lens Blur, we can not only dictate the degree of blur, but also define exactly where it occurs, enabling us to make creative adjustments with a live preview.

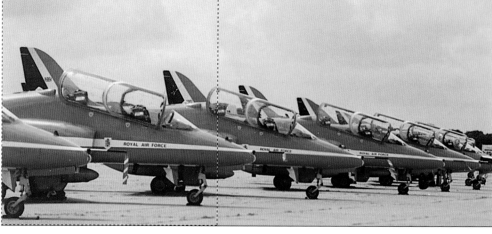

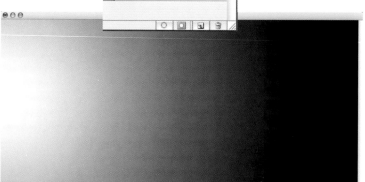

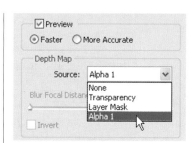

1 Begin by creating an Alpha channel as outlines in Method 2. Here, the picture of the jet aircraft has an alpha channel from a white-to-black gradient running from left to right.

2 Go to **Filter > Blur > Lens Blur**. While you can use the filter with a simple selection, using an Alpha channel enables you to determine the areas of focus and blur with a greater degree of control. To load an alpha channel, select it from the Depth Map Source drop-down.

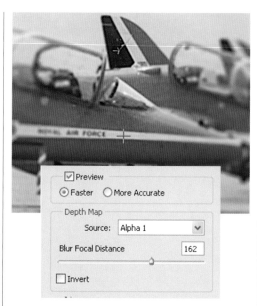

3 The Blur Focus Distance slider is this filter's biggest time-saver. The range of the slider is from 0 to 255, corresponding to the shades of gray from pure black (0) to pure white (255). This corresponds exactly to the shades in the Alpha channel, which goes from white on the left through shades of gray to black on the right. So if we position the slider at position 0, the pixels corresponding to the black area of the channel (The extreme right) will be focused. Conversely, positioning the slider at position 255 will keep the pixels in the white area (extreme left) of the channel in sharp focus. This means we can choose any single jet in the line-up to concentrate focus and gradually blur out the others. To set it, just click an area in the Preview window and this becomes the point of focus. For this image, click near the nose of the second jet from the left and the slider jumps to 162 automatically.

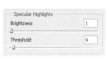

4 Now to the Specular Highlights. The Threshold setting determines which pixels will be treated as specular highlights—the bright white glints and reflections that occur on shiny surfaces or on the edges of objects. Any pixels brighter than this value will be treated as specular highlights, with the Brightness slider controlling their intensity.

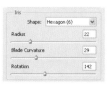

5 The blur's appearance is dictated by the Shape, which simulates the effects of the blades that create the aperture on a camera—the more blades, the more circular the iris becomes. The Radius setting determines the degree of blur, the Blade Curvature smoothes the edges of the iris, and the Rotation setting rotates the iris shape.

44

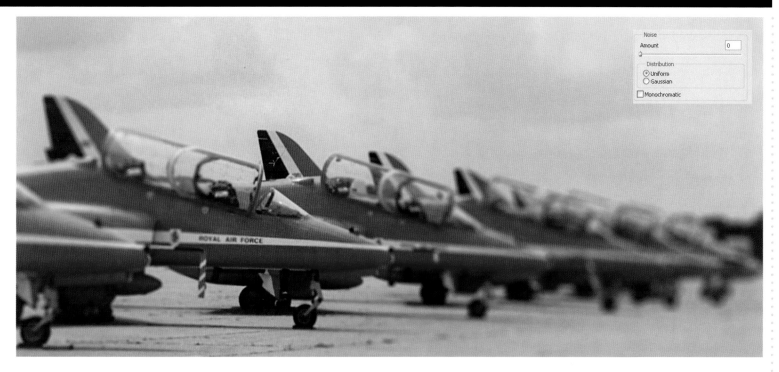

6 Finally, Noise can be added to replace any film grain that may become lost as a result of the blurring. If noise is added, it's best to be conservative with the Amount setting. Set the Distribution to Gaussian, and use monochromatic noise to avoid affecting color in the image. Here's the image with my choice of focus and blur applied.

EDITING THE ALPHA CHANNEL

The result using this method isn't always perfect. Some areas of the image that should be within the focal plane may be blurred, while other areas that should lie outside it remain in sharp focus. The trick here is to edit the Alpha mask. Undo the Lens Blur, then go to the Channels palette, and click on Alpha 1. Make one of the RGB channels visible so you can see what you are doing. Now use the Color Picker to sample colors from the gradient, then use those colors to paint on the Alpha channel in areas that should be on the same plane (i.e. at the same distance from the camera). With your new alpha channel finished, return to the image and reapply the Lens blur. The effect should now look more realistic.

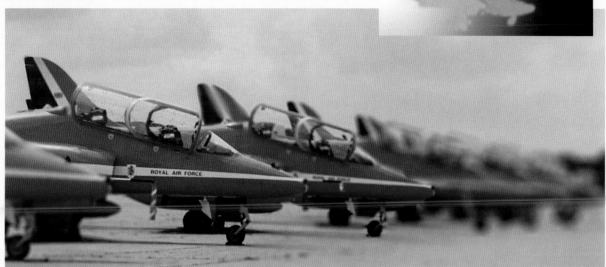

Motion blurring

apturing a fleeting moment on camera is one of the most satisfying aspects of photography, but this doesn't necessarily mean sharp focus and fine detail. Pin-sharp clarity suits a single drop of water hitting the still surface of a pond, but a slow exposure can turn a waterfall into a beautiful, shimmering blur. While sharp focus can freeze motion in time, blurring can create a powerful impression of movement. Photoshop's Motion Blur filter is designed with this in mind.

The Motion Blur filter

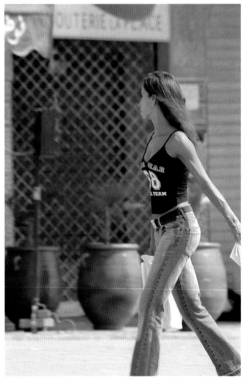

1 Using Motion Blur effectively takes a little preparation. Used straight on an image, it creates a loss of detail, or merely replicates the effect of camera shake. In this image, we want to preserve detail while creating a feeling of rapid motion.

2 To start, make a feathered selection of the rear half of the girl. A Feather setting of about 6 pixels should be sufficient for a low-resolution shot, but you need to use higher values for high-resolution images. Finish a "quick and dirty" selection—the blur effect means that accuracy isn't vital—then press Ctrl/Cmd + J to copy and paste it to a new layer. Call the new layer "copied selection."

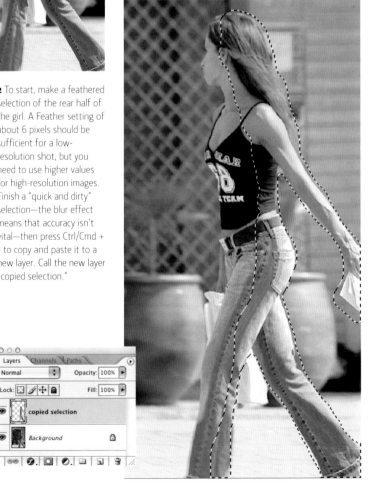

46

3 Keep the copied selection layer active and go to **Filter > Blur > Motion Blur**. Set the angle to o degrees and the distance to 90 pixels. Make sure the Move tool is selected, then press the right arrow key on the keyboard about 12 times to move the selection to the right. This gives the impression that the girl is leaving a blur of movement in her wake.

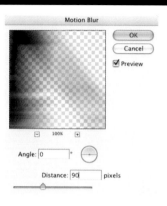

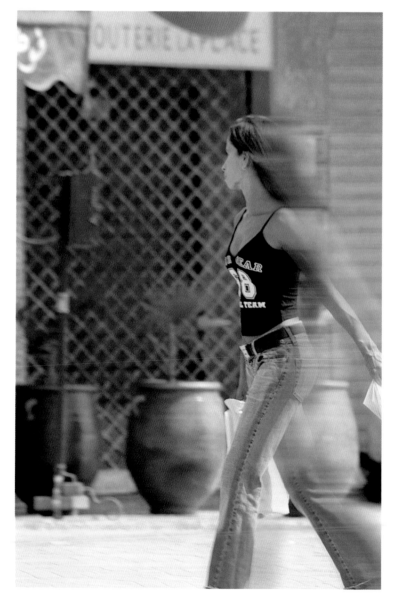

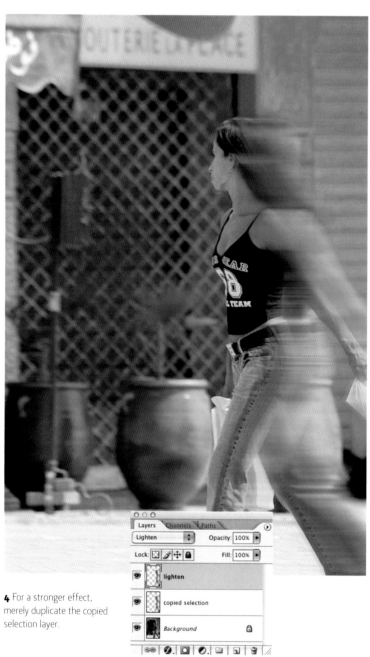

4 For a stronger effect, merely duplicate the copied selection layer.

TIP

BLURRING WITH BLEND MODES
After duplicating the copied selection layer, try changing the blend mode of the top version to Lighten. This produces an almost ghostly effect.

Motion blurring

The Radial Blur filter

The Radial Blur filter is another highly effective tool for suggesting movement. It simulates a popular effect used in conventional photography when taking pictures with a zoom lens. A relatively slow shutter speed is used, exposing the image as the lens is zoomed through its full focal length. The result, when successful, displays a focused centre with blurred lines emanating away from the central area—as if the viewer were looking down a tunnel. The picture of the four-wheel drive vehicle in the desert looks a little static, and we want to create the sense of drama and urgency associated with driving in a challenging environment. Using Radial Blur will help.

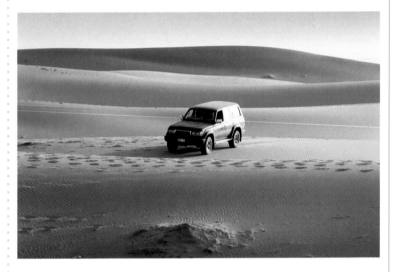

1 For maximum effect, images with strong contrast or lots of color work best. This generates a strong streak effect, which accentuates the sense of motion. In this example, a high contrast effect is required. Press Ctrl+L (Win)/ Cmd + L (Mac) to bring up the Levels dialog box, then increase the contrast by bringing the black and white input markers closer together. The impact is clear in the foreground, where the heightened definition is perfect for Radial Blur.

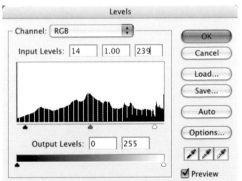

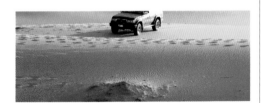

2 Now duplicate the background layer and rename it "Blur." Activate the duplicate layer and go to **Filter > Blur > Radial Blur**. Set the Blur Method to Zoom, Quality to Best, and the Amount to 38. Move the centre point of the blur by clicking in the location indicated in the Blur Center window. This will place the centre roughly in the middle front of the vehicle. If you don't get it right first time, just Undo the effect and click again in a slightly different location.

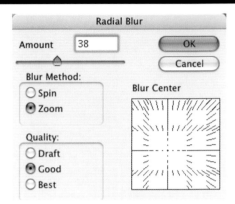

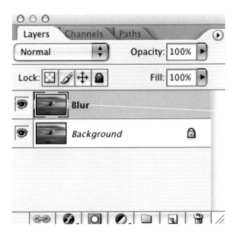

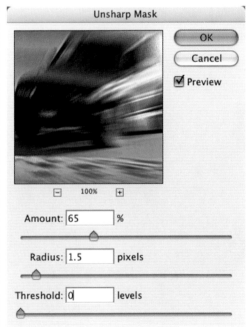

3 The chosen Amount setting creates the feel of movement without destroying the clarity of the image, but the effect needs a little sharpening for maximum impact. Go to **Filter > Sharpen > Unsharp Mask** and apply the settings shown.

48

4 Finally, the original background needs to be re-established. Add a layer mask to the Blur layer by clicking on the layer mask icon, second from left at the bottom of the Layers palette. When you've finished painting on the layer mask (see left), the result should look like this.

ADDING THE LAYER MASK

Painting on the mask with black paint reveals the details of the layer below (the sharper details of the original sky and the dunes on the horizon), while white paints the Blur layer back in again. The mask appears as a thumbnail on the layers palette, but you can check its extent using two easy options: Option-click (Mac) or Alt-click (Windows) on the layer mask thumbnail to view only the mask, or Option-Shift-click/Alt-Shift-click to see it as a colored overlay.

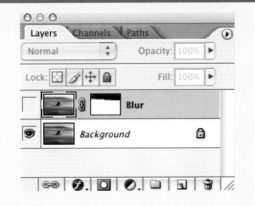

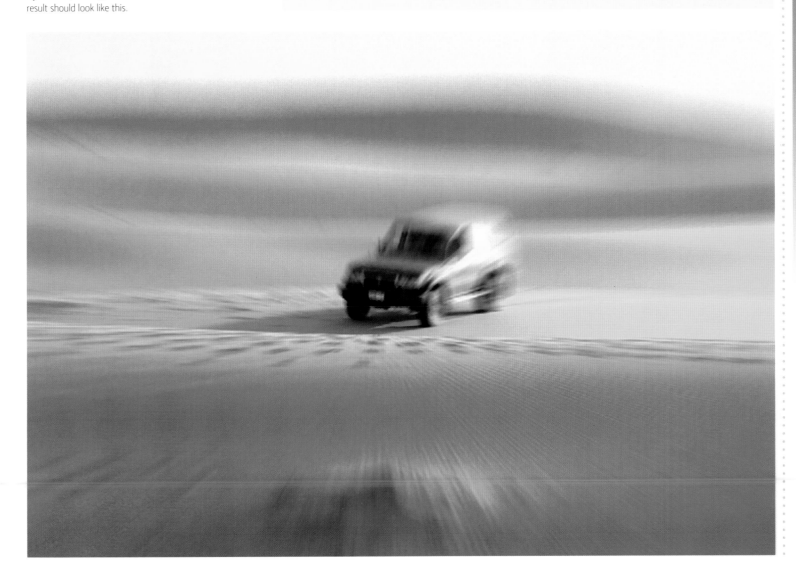

RETOUCHING PORTRAITS

Removing red eye & changing hair color

Whitening teeth & eyes

Enhancing lips

Changing hair color

Removing skin blemishes & wrinkles

Perfecting skin tones

Reshaping faces

Removing red eye & changing eye color

While it's unlikely to be a concern in studio portraiture, red eye is a regular problem in snapshots of people. The phenomenon is a consequence of a flash mounted close to the lens reflecting back from the subject's retina. It can be eliminated by using a flash that isn't mounted to the camera or by using an in-camera red eye reduction system, and it can also be dealt with after shooting, using Photoshop. As a bonus, the techniques used for red eye removal can also be employed to change eye color for cosmetic effect.

Method 1: **The Red Eye Tool**

Photoshop CS2 users can save time and effort by using the new Red Eye tool. It's found in the Toolbox, in the same section as the Healing Brush and the Spot Healing Brush.

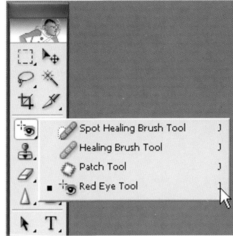

1 First, select the Red Eye Tool from the Toolbox. A crosshair pointer will appear: drag this to form a rough rectangle over the area that contains the pupil. It doesn't need to be very accurate, but it must encompass the whole pupil.

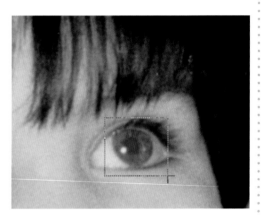

2 The software will automatically identify the red area of the pupil and darken it. Repeat this process to fix all of the other red eyes in the photo.

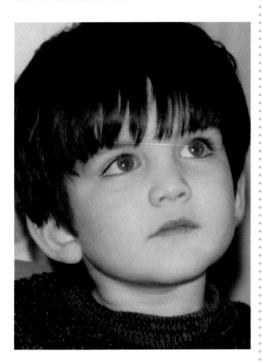

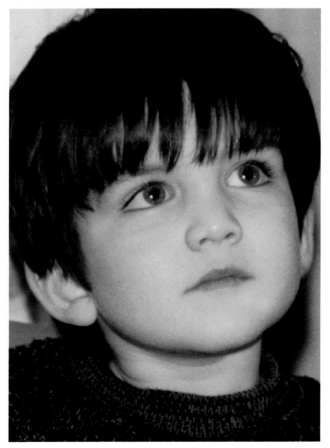

Method 2: **Color Balance with selections**

Users of Photoshop CS and older versions will have to employ another technique. Luckily, this method is virtually automatic.

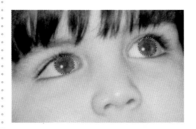

1 First, select the Elliptical Marquee tool and make a feathered selection of the pupils of the eyes. Press Ctrl/Cmd + B to bring up the Color Balance dialog box.

2 Red is the offending color, so select Midtones from the Tone Balance radio buttons and drag the Cyan/Red slider to the left until the red is decreased in most of the pupils. The red will still be visible in the dark centre of the pupil, so change the Tone Balance to Shadows, and drag the Cyan/Red slider to the left to further reduce the red.

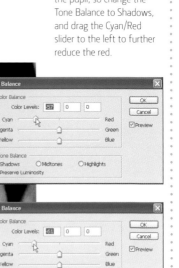

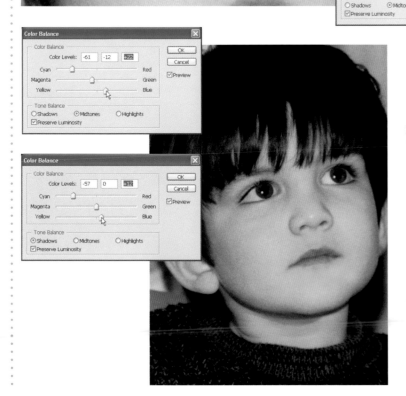

Method 3: **Selective color**

If you want to change the eye color completely, you can make radical adjustments using the Selective Color tool. Make a selection around the iris then go to **Image > Adjustments > Selective Color**.

1 Select Neutrals from the Color drop-down and set the Method to Absolute. This results in a pronounced effect which is perfect for our aims. The settings applied here increase the cyan significantly, which counters the red, reduces the levels of magenta and (to a lesser extent) yellow, and results in a piercing blue. The final color and intensity can be fine-tuned by making small adjustments to the sliders.

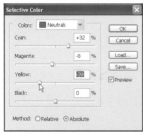

3 In this example, because the red was so extensive, it required a major shift in hue to completely remove it, but this has resulted in an unnatural green cast. To compensate, select Midtones and drag the Magenta/Green slider to the left to reduce the green, then drag the Yellow/Blue slider to the right to add a little blue. Finally select the Shadows and drag the Yellow/Blue slider to the right. This technique allows for lot of creative interpretation of the eye color in addition to removing red eye.

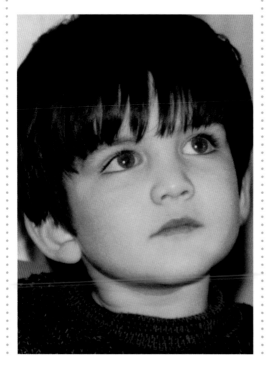

Whitening teeth & eyes

Whenever the need arises to make a natural element white or whiter, it's tempting to set the foreground color to white and reach for the airbrush. This works if applied with care, but it's easier to achieve a more realistic effect using other Photoshop tools. Here, a small amount of whitening applied to the model's teeth and eyes will lift the whole image.

Method 1: **Dodge**

The first technique successfully whitens your teeth without placing demands on your brushwork. As with most retouching tasks, it's best to work on a duplicate layer in case you make a mistake.

1 Create the new layer, select the Dodge tool, then go to the Tool Options bar and set the Range to Midtones. The default Exposure setting is 50%, which is a good starting point. Now run the Dodge tool over the teeth until they look whiter. The Dodge tool is very powerful, so more than three brush strokes could leave the teeth looking overdone. If that's the case, use Undo (Ctrl/Cmd +Z) to step back, then reduce the Exposure setting in the Tool Options before returning to work.

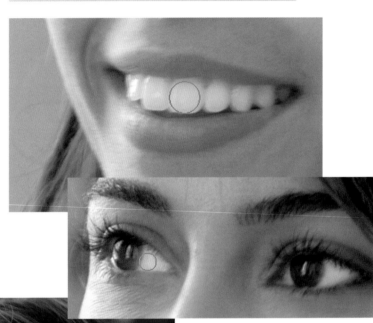

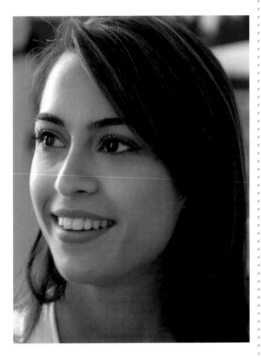

2 Work over the eyes in the same way, zooming out often to get a look at the image as a whole. The close-up view can often be misleading.

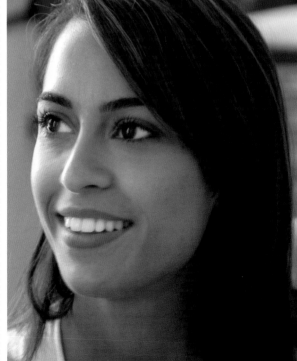

54

Method 2: **Screen mode**

If you're not comfortable with applying brush strokes for whitening, there are other options. In this technique, all you need to do by hand is to make a selection around the areas to be retouched. This technique works equally well with teeth or the whites of eyes.

1 Press Ctrl/Cmd + J to copy and paste the selection to a new layer, called "teeth." Change the new teeth layer's blend mode to Screen.

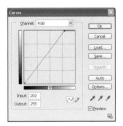

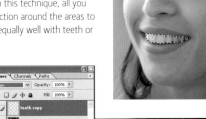

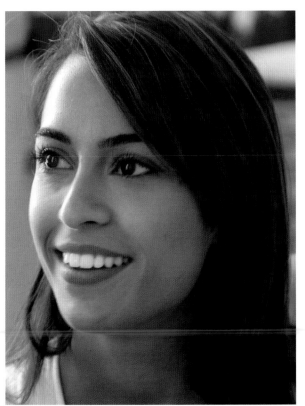

2 This effect is too strong in itself, but by reducing the layer's opacity you have complete control over the degree of whitening. The next example shows the layer opacity set to 60%.

Method 3: **Curves**

We can also use Curves to brighten the teeth and change their color. This method is particularly useful if you want to fine-tune the effect in more detail.

1 Make another selection of the teeth, then choose **Image > Adjustments > Curves** (Ctrl/Cmd + M). We need a white adjustment, so keep the Channel set to RGB and drag the top right corner of the diagonal line to the left as shown.

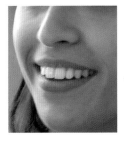

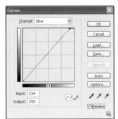

2 You'll notice that this results in a slight yellowing of the teeth. Blue is the complement of yellow, so pick the Blue channel from the Channel drop-down, then create the curve as shown. To copy mine exactly, click on the top endpoint of the curve, then type 234 in the Input number field. (For a full explanation on using Levels and Curves to control color, see pages 26-27.) The final image shows the same settings applied to the whites of the eyes.

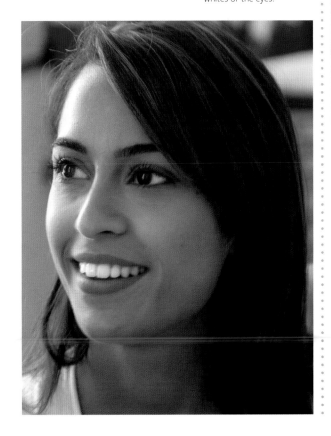

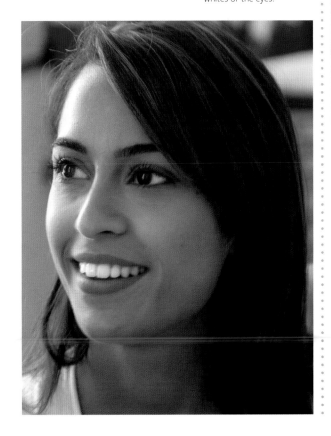

55

Enhancing lips

As with eyes, the first resort of the novice Photoshop retouch artist is to slap a brushload of scarlet on the model's lips. However, a more sophisticated approach will pay dividends when the style awards are handed out. In this example, the model's lips are quite muted in color and the surface is almost completely matte.

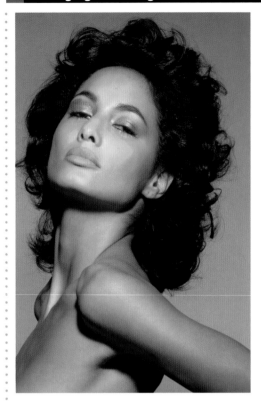

Adding a glamorous gloss

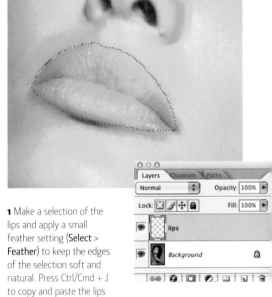

1 Make a selection of the lips and apply a small feather setting (**Select > Feather**) to keep the edges of the selection soft and natural. Press Ctrl/Cmd + J to copy and paste the lips selection to a new layer. Rename it "lips."

2 There are several options to boost the color of the lips, but the Selective Color command is particularly flexible. Go to **Image > Adjustments > Selective Color**. Choose Reds from the drop-down and enable the Absolute radio button. Applying the settings as shown will generate a strong pink color.

Selective Color

Colors: Reds

Cyan: -23 %
Magenta: 21 %
Yellow: -6 %
Black: 0 %

OK
Cancel
Load...
Save...
☑ Preview

Method: ○ Relative ● Absolute

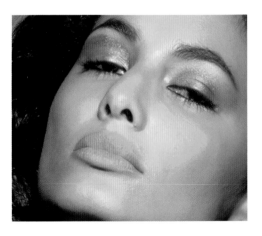

3 To change the pink to a luscious red and bring out the underlying texture, change the Lips layer's blend mode to Color Burn. The gloss still needs emphasizing. Press Ctrl/Cmd + M to bring up the Curves dialog box and apply the curve in the example to create a realistic wet look.

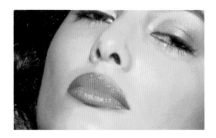

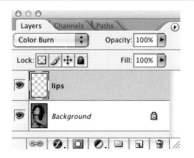

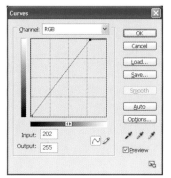

4 The last stage adds a few highlights—essential for the Hollywood studio glamour shot effect. Create a new layer called "highlights" at the top of the Layers palette. Activate the new layer, then paint over the natural highlight areas of the lips with a small paintbrush using 50% gray.

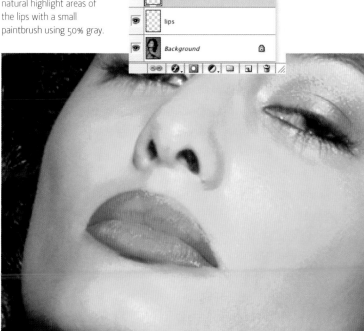

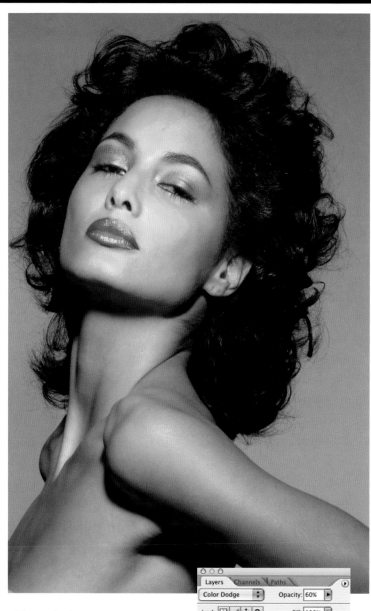

5 When you're done, change the layer's blend mode to Color Dodge. The highlights will look much brighter, creating a slightly overdone, high-gloss effect. For the sake of realism, reduce the opacity of the Highlights layer to approximately 60%.

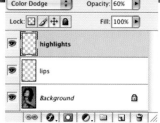

Changing hair color

Converting blonde hair to dark hair in Photoshop is easy, but how about making very dark hair into a realistic blonde? It's certainly more demanding, but it is possible, and we can even define what kind of blonde tone to create. Lightening the dark brown hair of this model is a case in point.

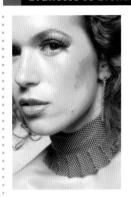

Brunette to blonde

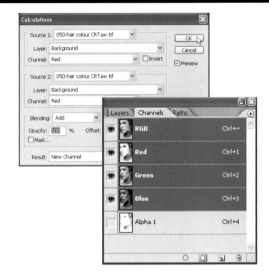

1 As a starting point, we need to lose the heavy dark shades of the hair but keep all of the texture. Go to **Image > Calculations**. The drop-down boxes for sources 1 and 2 should be identical, with both using the background layer of the same document and the red channel. Set the Blending drop-down to Add and the Result drop-down box to New Channel. Click the Channels tab and you will see a new channel called "Alpha 1" has been created.

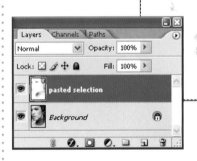

2 The newly created channel must now be copied and pasted as a new layer. Click the Alpha 1 channel to activate it, then press Ctrl/Cmd + A to select all and Ctrl/Cmd + C to copy. Click the RGB composite channel, then return to the layers palette and press Ctrl/Cmd + V to paste the selection as a new layer above the background layer. Call it "pasted selection."

3 We now have a neutral black-and-white canvas on which to paint. Select the Paintbrush from the toolbox and set the brush mode to Color from the tool options bar. Use a large, soft-edged brush (125 pixels in this case), and choose a yellow color as the foreground color (you can always use the eyedropper to sample an actual blonde shade from another image). The color I'm using here is R229 G232 B138. Paint over the entire hair area. Don't worry if you spill over onto the skin area a little, as we can deal with that later.

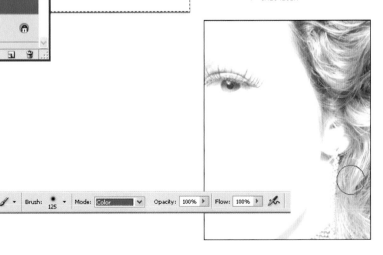

4 When all the hair is painted, add a layer mask to the pasted selection layer, set to Reveal All. Paint on the mask with black to reveal the all of the original background layer with the exception of the hair.

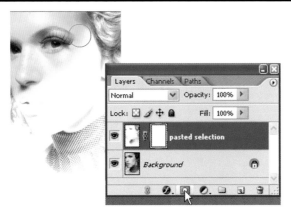

If you are looking for a different blonde color, the Adjustment Layer gives us the flexibility we need to simulate different shades. To create a strawberry blonde, add some red. For a platinum blonde, add some blue. Remember, the Tone Balance radio buttons allow you to change the shadows and highlights for more pronounced effects, but for authenticity keep the effect subtle.

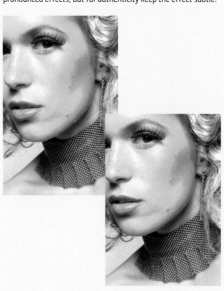

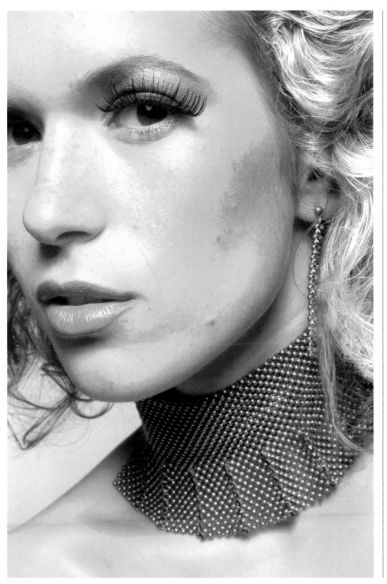

5 At this stage the image probably looks like the result of a disastrous trip to the hair parlor. The color is too strong to look natural. Even sampling an actual blond shade would have this effect. Luckily, the first choice of color isn't critical. Go to **Layer** > **New Adjustment Layer** > **Color Balance** to create a Color Balance adjustment layer. Check the option to ensure a clipping mask is made between it and the painted hair layer.

6 The Color Balance dialog box offers more control over the final shade of blonde. The main problem is that the current choice of yellow is too green, so we compensate by dragging the Magenta/Green slider to the left (to about –60). Keep the Midtones radio button enabled. This will transform the model's hair into a more natural blonde color.

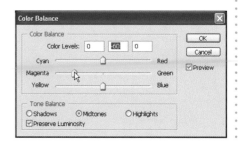

Removing skin blemishes & wrinkles

If you are a reader of popular women's magazines you might be forgiven for believing that the glowing faces that grace the front covers all possess the most perfect satiny skin. Sadly, this is an illusion. Perfect skin does not exist; at least not over the duration of a lifetime. But while imperfection is a part of life, you can still sell the illusion with a little Photoshop magic.

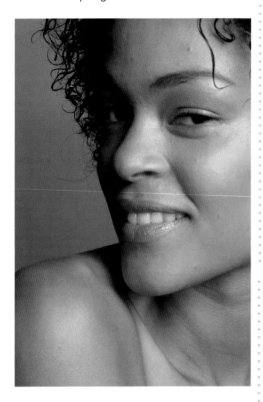

Removing individual marks

This model has certain blemishes that can easily be removed. For isolated blemishes, the Healing Brush offers the fastest and least destructive method of removal.

1 Select the Healing Brush, go to the Tool Options bar, and set the Source to Sampled. The tool will now copy the texture from the area first sampled, while retaining the current color and brightness values.

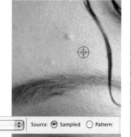

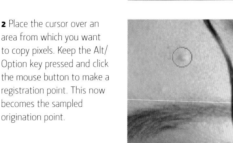

2 Place the cursor over an area from which you want to copy pixels. Keep the Alt/Option key pressed and click the mouse button to make a registration point. This now becomes the sampled origination point.

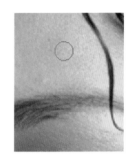

3 Now place the cursor over the blemish requiring removal and click to paint out the offending area. In this instance one click will suffice, provided the size of the brush is big enough to cover the blemish. The great thing about the Healing Brush—unlike the older Clone Stamp tool—is that it matches the texture, shading, lighting and transparency of the original subject, making the edit seamless in all but the most difficult of situations.

Tip

SPOT HEALING BRUSH
Photoshop CS2 supplements the Healing Brush with a new Spot Healing Brush. This tool makes an intelligent guess at the texture it should use to cover the blemish, meaning that there is no need to Alt/Opt-click on a sample point first!

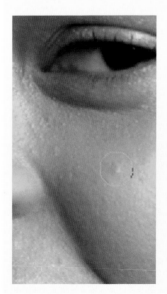
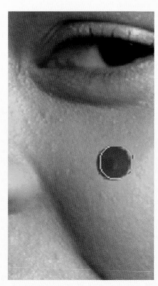
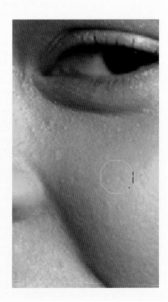

Smoothing wrinkles

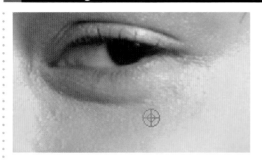 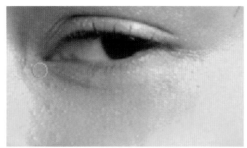

The healing brush is also an excellent tool for removing lines and wrinkles even where the skin tone varies greatly.

1 First, make a registration point by Alt/Option-clicking under the heavy line below the eye.

2 Now drag the brush over the heavy line. While dragging, the color being painted may appear quite different, as it literally clones the pixels from the sampled area onto the new area. However, on releasing the mouse button, the necessary shade and texture adjustments will be made to give a seamless result.

Multiple blemishes

Although highly effective, the healing brush requires a separate action for each element to be removed. This is not a problem when there are only one or two areas requiring attention, but it can become time-consuming for multiple blemishes covering a wider area. On page 76 we look at using the Patch tool as a method for hiding unwanted areas—a method that works well as long there is an area big enough from which to copy replacement pixels. This may not always be possible on a person's face, so instead we will use a less obvious technique.

1 First, make feathered selections of the areas where more than one blemish exist.

2 Now go to Filter>Noise>Dust and Scratches. As the name suggests, this filter is associated more commonly with cleaning up scans and old images, but don't let that put you off. Set the Threshold to 9, as this allows some of the skin texture to show through. If the threshold is too low, the area becomes too smooth and looks false. Set the Radius to 21, but gauge this by eye, increasing the value until the unwanted blemishes fade away. The end result is the appearance of blemish-free skin, without losing that all-important texture.

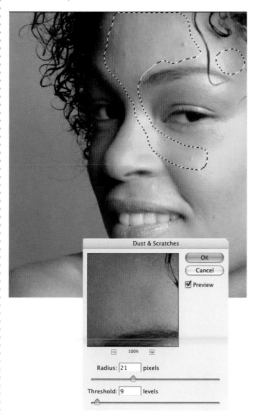

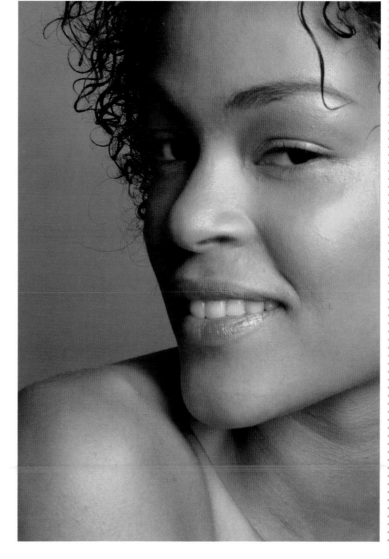

Perfecting skin tones

hiny faces are the bugbear of make-up artists in film, TV and still photography. Walk into any studio and you will see them furiously damping down shiny foreheads, noses, and any other glowing features. You might not have access to these facilities, but when there isn't a make-up artist to intervene, Photoshop can work wonders.

Removing shine

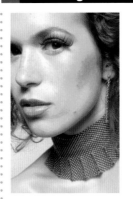

The shine on this model's face spoils the shot over quite a broad area. Fortunately, it's possible to fix the problem with one easy correction.

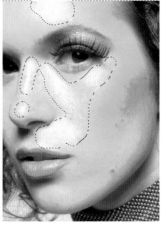

1 Make a feathered selection of the shiny area to be fixed. This image has a low 72ppi resolution, so a Feather setting of 8 pixels works well.

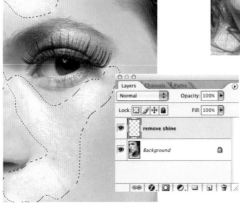

2 With the selection still active, create a new layer called "remove shine." Next, use the eyedropper to sample a midtone of the skin. The color I'm using is R255, G182, B144.

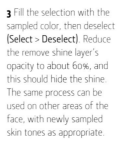

3 Fill the selection with the sampled color, then deselect (Select > Deselect). Reduce the remove shine layer's opacity to about 60%, and this should hide the shine. The same process can be used on other areas of the face, with newly sampled skin tones as appropriate.

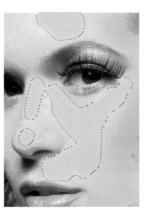

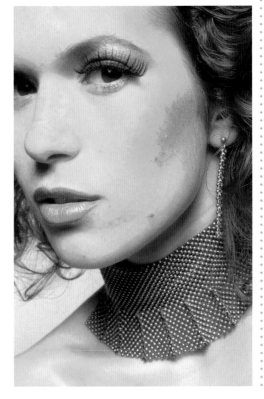

62

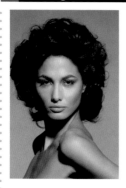

Conversely, a skin tone that is too flat can look dead and lifeless, so we can also use Photoshop to add highlights. Placed strategically, these can transform the face and draw attention away from any less flattering characteristics, should they exist.

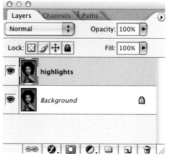

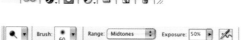

1 For this method, work on a duplicate layer. Create one and call it "highlights." This allows us to make adjustments if necessary in the final stages. Select the Dodge tool from the Toolbox, setting up the Tool Options as shown.

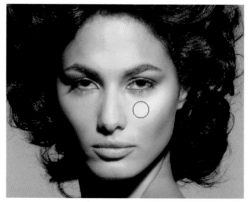

2 Drag the tool over the cheekbones to enhance the existing muted highlight. If the effect is too strong, try reducing the Dodge tool's Exposure setting. You will achieve more realistic and controllable results by applying a number of strokes at lower Exposure settings.

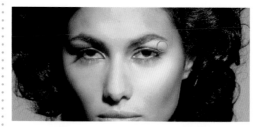

3 Repeat the process above the eye, below the eyebrow, then do the same with the other side of the face. Dabbing with the Dodge tool over the natural highlight of the chin and along the shoulder and arm also adds more definition.

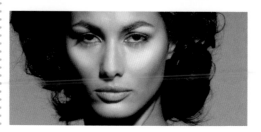

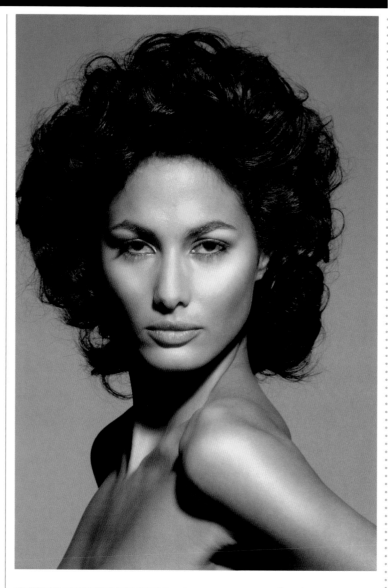

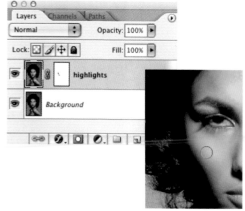

4 If you have gone too far with any of the highlights, fine-tune them by adding a Layer Mask set to Reveal All to the highlights layer. Here the highlight on the model's right cheekbone is too bold, so, using a soft-edged brush at about 40% opacity, paint on the mask with black to reveal more of the original layer below. This gives you complete control over the intensity of the added highlights, enabling you to create a polished final result.

Reshaping faces

The Liquify filter provides an intuitive method for resculpting faces and bodies in general. Applied methodically, the edits can be completely indiscernible, and it can even be used in a subtle fashion to change a person's expression. For this example, we'll apply two different methods from within the Liquify dialog box.

Method 1: **Warp**

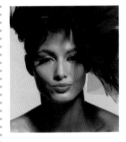

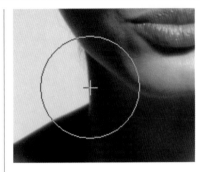

For this example, we'll apply two different methods from within the Liquify dialog box.

1 Go to **Filter** > **Liquify**. Select the Warp tool (the first tool in the filter's Toolbox). Go to the settings on the right, and set the Size of the brush to roughly cover the size of the area to be affected. The idea here is to slim the jawline. To change the brush size as you work, use the square bracket keys: [will reduce the size;] will increase it.

2 The other two relevant settings are Brush Density and Brush Pressure. The Brush Density defines the feathering at the edge of the brush—the effect of the brush is more pronounced at the centre than at the edge. Brush Pressure affects the speed at which the distortion is made. You can set it to maximum, but if you are new to the tool, it's often better to reduce the pressure and watch the results at a slower pace. Place the crosshair of the brush on the left edge of the face, then click and drag to the right until you get the desired results. If you go too far, press Ctrl/Cmd + Z to undo and try again.

3 In this example, the neck bulges out in a strange way just below the jaw. Repeat the process outlined in Step 2 to streamline it.

4 Do the same on the other side of the face and neck. Click OK and that's it. Compare the final image with the starting image and you'll see a radical difference that looks completely natural.

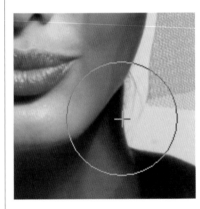

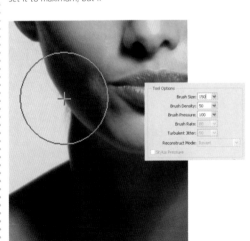

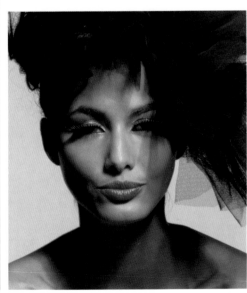

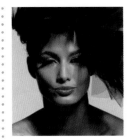

The second method uses the Liquify Pucker tool.

1 When you're editing symmetrically, as here, it often helps to use a grid. Go to the View Options area of the Liquify dialog box and enable the Show Mesh checkbox. Set the Mesh Size to large and the Mesh Color to something that contrasts with the image.

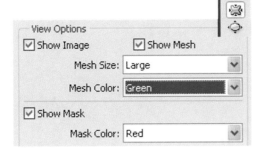

2 Increase the Brush Size to cover most of the bottom left corner of the face. Here I'm using size 270 on a 72ppi file. Place the crosshair of the brush on a horizontal line of the grid and count about 3 or 4 squares to the right of the edge of the face. The example shows where I have placed the cursor. Click 2 or 3 times. The number of clicks needed will change according to the amount of thinning desired.

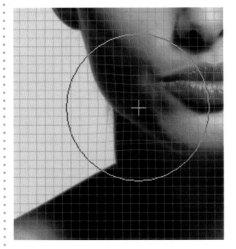

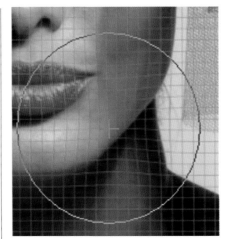

3 Keep the cursor aligned on the same horizontal gridline and move to the other side of the face. Let the cursor rest about 3 or 4 squares in from the right edge of the face and click again to pucker the area.

4 Reduce the size of the pucker brush and the brush pressure, then run the cursor down the edges of the neck where it bulges out. As you drag, the neck will conform to the run of the cursor. You will find this process easier with the grid switched off. Lowering the brush pressure slows down the distortion, giving you more time to control your hand movement. It's a tricky maneuver, and it may take a few attempts to get a feel for it. The final effect is less obvious than with the previous method, but both require a practiced hand to get a realistic result.

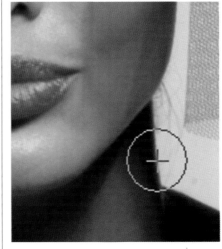

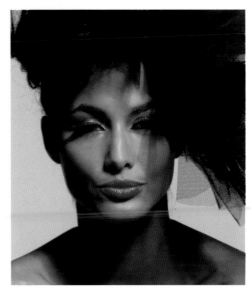

65

RETOUCHING LANDSCAPES

Interesting skies

Extending image areas

Removing unwanted areas

Correcting perspective

Interesting skies

The sky is one of the landscape photographer's greatest assets. A natural backdrop, it provides a subtle canvas that binds a composition together, or it can be a bold visual statement on its own. Yet many landscape shots are discarded because the sky is too light, too dark, or just too boring. Thankfully, with Photoshop even the most nondescript sky can be easily transformed into a beautiful patchwork of light and color.

Darkening skies

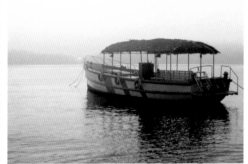

One of the major causes of lackluster landscapes is exposure. While, correctly exposing for the sky creates a gloomy, indistinct landscape in the foreground, exposing for the landscape means the brighter sky is washed out of the image. This shot is a typical example.

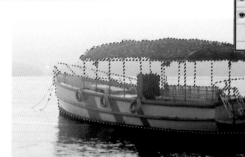

1 We are not going to make any adjustments to the boat at this stage, so the first thing to do is make a selection of it and place it out of harm's way. Use the Extract tool, or the selection tool of your choice. With the selection completed, press Ctrl/Cmd + J to copy and paste it to a new layer. Rename it "Boat."

2 Now duplicate the background layer (use Ctrl/Cmd + J again, since, with no live selection, the whole current active layer is duplicated). Rename the layer "sky" and change its blend mode to Multiply. This darkens the image, but the boat isn't affected as it's isolated on its own layer at the top of the stack.

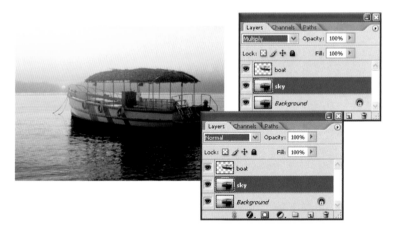

3 Rather than leave the photo there, we can create a richer sunset with just a few more steps. Add a Curves adjustment layer to the sky layer (Layer > New Adjustment Layer) and, in the Curves dialog box, drag the curve down from the centre to gradually darken the sky and water further.

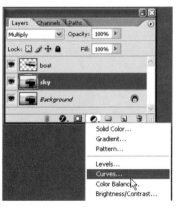

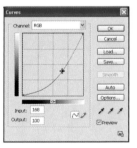

4 The darkened sky works better, but it has made the roof and bow of the boat look too light to be real. To remedy this, run the Burn tool over the affected area of the boat layer. Use a large brush with the Burn tool set to Midtones at 65% opacity.

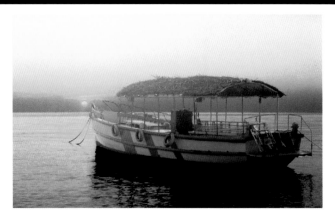 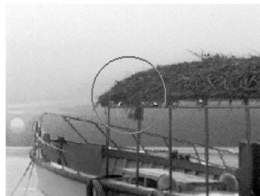

5 Finally, we'll darken the sky a little more, enriching the color to give a soft pink/orange glow. Activate the sky layer and go to **Select > Color Range**, then choose Highlights from the Select drop-down. This action selects the highlights in the layer, including most of the sky and the lighter parts of the water.

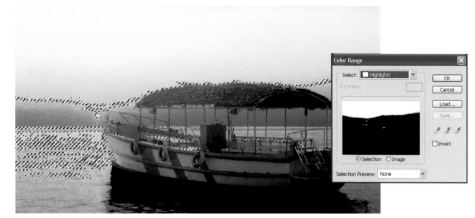

6 A quick and easy fix for a richer color is to go to **Image > Adjustments > Hue/Saturation** (Ctrl/Cmd + U). You can also use the Hue/Saturation command as an adjustment layer (as with the Curves previously). The settings shown result in a desirable orange glow: a big improvement on the original pale sky. And with the adjustment layers in place, you can always change the Hue and Brightness settings if you change your mind later.

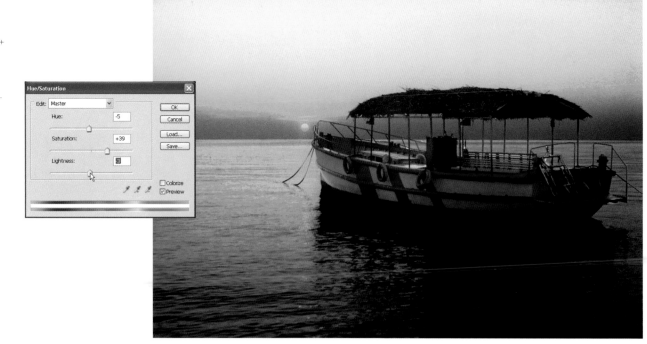

Interesting skies

Lightening skies

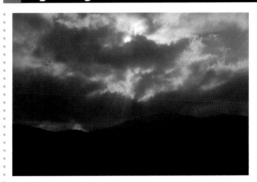

Washed-out skies are dull, but a dark sky can be just as uninteresting. For this example, both the sky and the hills below need more light and contrast, but this treatment could also destroy the drama of the scene. Luckily, there are ways to avoid this.

1 First duplicate the background layer (Ctrl/Cmd + J) and change the duplicate layer's blend mode to Screen. This immediately lightens the sky, and also reveals detail in the hills and lifts the heaviness of the clouds. However, it also washes out the highlights.

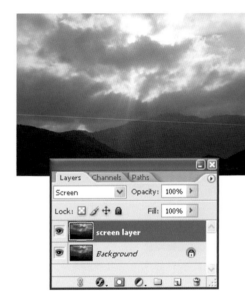

3 So far, so good, but the developing image has an unflattering gray cast, and has also lost some vital contrast. To remedy this, add a Levels adjustment layer to the luminosity layer. Be sure that it's clipped to the luminosity layer as a clipping mask. When the Levels dialog box opens, make a small adjustment to the White and gray markers, moving both very slightly to the right to darken the pixels.

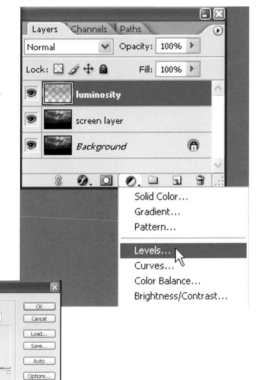

2 To re-establish the highlights without affecting the shadows, we need to make a luminosity mask. If you're using Windows press Ctrl + Alt + Shift + ~. On a Mac press Cmd + Alt + ~. The result is a selection of the highlights in the layer, based on their luminosity. Press Ctrl/Cmd + J to copy this selection to a new layer, then change the new layer's blend mode back to Normal. We now have a lighter sky and hills area without blown-out highlights.

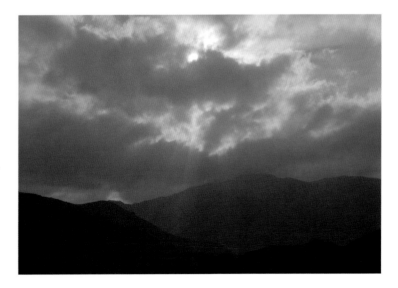

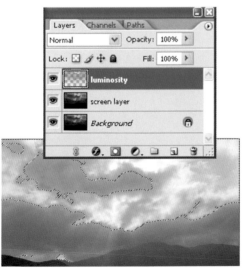

4 Now select the Blue channel from the Channel drop-down and boost the blues in the image by dragging the White and Gray markers to the left. This replaces the dull gray cast with a livelier blue tint, while bumping up the contrast. Together, these changes brighten the sky.

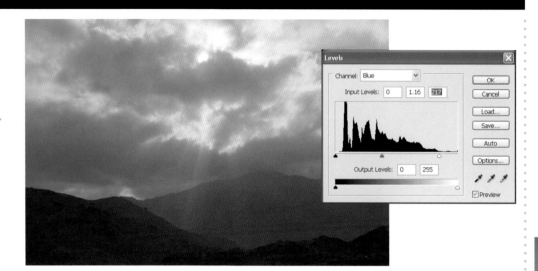

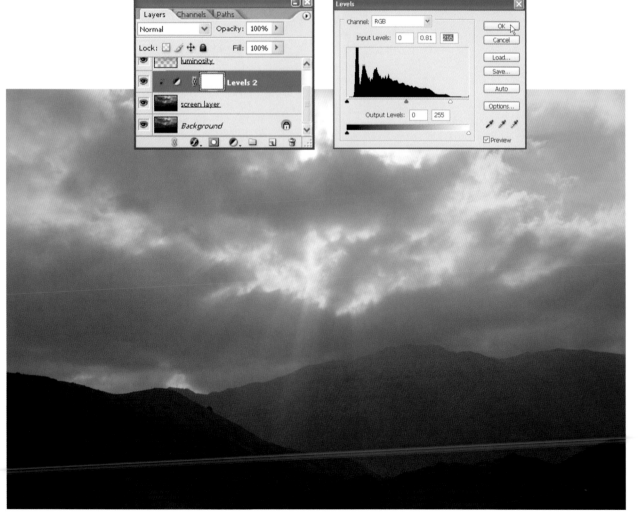

5 One final step enables us to fine-tune the contrast between the sky and hills. Add a Levels adjustment layer to the sky layer, again making a clipping mask between the two layers. Now slide the White marker slightly to the left and the Gray marker slightly to the right to strengthen tonal contrast in the affected pixels. The change is subtle, but the improved contrast is enough to strengthen the image considerably.

Interesting skies

Creating skies

The previous techniques work well provided you have some sky to work on, but they're no good if you just have a featureless, colorless space. In this case, it's time to call on artistic license, and make your own. There are two ways to go about this. You can either commandeer an existing sky from another image or you can make one, working—literally—from the ground up.

1 The image we are using fits into this hopeless category, so something new is called for. Make a selection of the sky, and save it as an alpha channel for later use (**Select > Save Selection**).

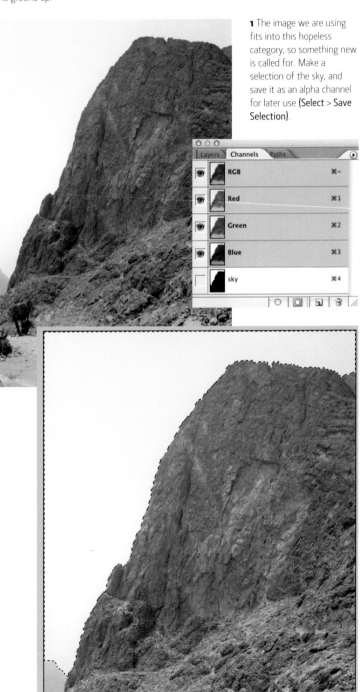

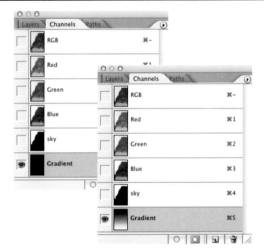

2 We want our digital sky to look real. A common cloudscape features random clouds at altitude, and these gradually diminish and become flatter and more uniform nearer the horizon. The next step creates this gradual fading effect. Go to the Layers palette, select the Channels tab, click on the arrow at the right side of the palette to access the flyout menu, and select New Channel. Call it "Gradient." Fill the channel with a black to white linear gradient running from top to bottom.

3 Load the sky channel as a selection by pressing Ctrl/Cmd + clicking the channel in the Channels palette. Now, subtract the gradient channel selection from the sky selection. This results in a new selection of the sky with a gradual fade towards the horizon. The beauty of this technique will become apparent in a moment. Press Ctrl/Cmd + Alt + click the gradient channel in the Channels palette. Notice the cursor now has a minus sign to show a subtraction will be made. At the moment, we can't see where the selection fades out, but all will become clear when we make some clouds.

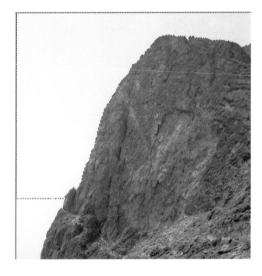

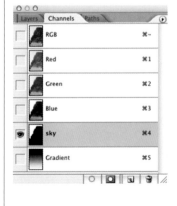

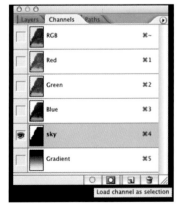

Load channel as selection

72

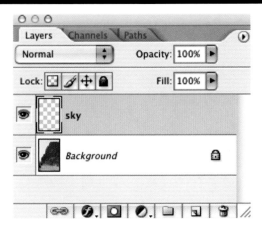

4 Create a new layer called "sky." Set up the foreground and background colors with a blue and white. These colors will form the basis for the sky.

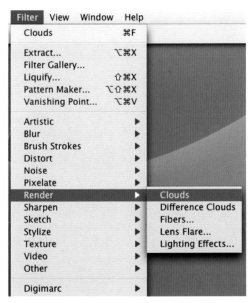

73

TIP

For a more pronounced effect, hold down the Alt/Opt key as you apply the Clouds filter. Alternatively, you can reapply the Clouds filter, as the effect becomes cumulative.

5 With the sky layer selected go to **Filter > Render > Clouds.** Notice how the depth and texture is concentrated towards the top of the image. Closer towards the horizon the effect is more subdued, as this is where the selection fades from black to white, thereby limiting the effect of the Clouds filter.

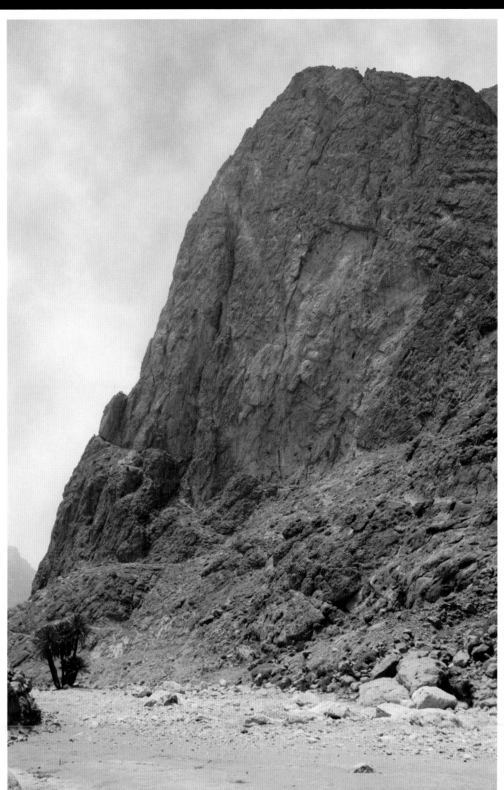

Extending image areas

Landscapes often reward a more panoramic widescreen approach, but your choices may be limited by the shots you've taken or the lenses used. To fill a larger area or make a landscape wider without making it any taller, there are ways of extending the scene by adding new, digital elements to the scene. The success of the process has much to do with the image in question. Extending a textureless, flat, green meadow isn't a problem, but an image filled with different colors and objects can be more demanding.

Method 1: **Cloning**

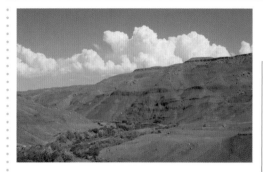

This method is the easiest, particularly if you're only creating a small extension and the shot isn't heavy on detail.

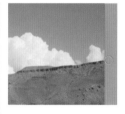

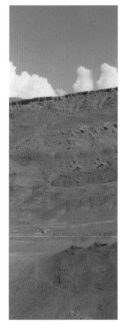

1 Increase the size of the canvas to the new target size by going to **Image > Canvas Size**. We'll add 50 pixels to the Width. Enter 1250 as the new total width size in the Width box. Click the square in the anchor diagram as shown to add the canvas to the right edge only. The canvas color, which is set as the background color in the Tools palette, is red for this example, just so you can see where the extra canvas appears.

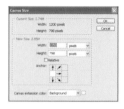

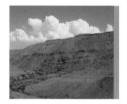

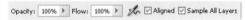

2 Now, select the Clone Stamp from the toolbox, then go to the Tool Options bar to paint at 100% opacity with Aligned and Use All Layers enabled.

3 Create a new layer and call it "clone." Although this isn't absolutely necessary it makes the effect easier to edit later. Activate the layer, and position the cursor on a point from which to start cloning pixels. I'm using the horizon, as this is a key area when you want the original image and the extension to line up accurately. When the cursor is in place, keep the Alt/Option key pressed down and click to make a registration point.

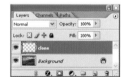

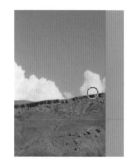

4 Now position the cursor in the red area parallel to the registration point, and start to paint until the red area is covered.

5 You may notice a problem with the cloned cloud. It is obviously a duplicate and looks false. We can disguise this by using the Clone Stamp. Alt + click to make a new registration point in the middle of one of the clouds, then cloning areas of the cloud to fill the blue gap. With just a few clicks of the mouse the cloud seems much more natural.

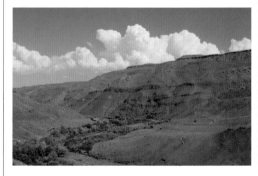

For large areas, we can try an alternative technique, copying part of the image to a new layer, then dragging that layer into a new position.

1 This time, we've extended the canvas out to 1352 pixels. This is greater than the width required, but the surplus allows for some maneuverability when positioning the duplicate. Make a rectangular selection of the area to be duplicated, and press Ctrl/Cmd + J to copy and paste the selection to a new layer. Call it "copied selection."

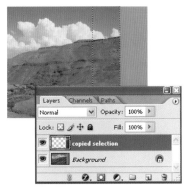

2 Position the copied selection layer so it lines up with the background. Use the horizon again as a reference point. Look for areas that line up naturally, if they exist. In this example, I've been able to line up two clouds that look as if they belong together.

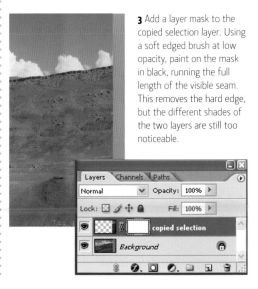

3 Add a layer mask to the copied selection layer. Using a soft edged brush at low opacity, paint on the mask in black, running the full length of the visible seam. This removes the hard edge, but the different shades of the two layers are still too noticeable.

4 This can be fixed with a simple gamma adjustment. Make sure the copied selection layer's image thumbnail is active (not the mask thumbnail). Press Ctrl/Cmd + L to bring up the Levels dialog box. Drag the Gamma (gray) slider to the right a short distance until the shades match. Finally, use the Crop tool to crop away the surplus areas at the right and bottom of the image.

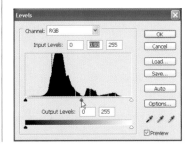

TIP

If you want to avoid any obvious signs of repetition in your extended landscape, try using the Healing Brush to remove some of the features. Brushing out the odd rock here and there can dramatically improve the finished result.

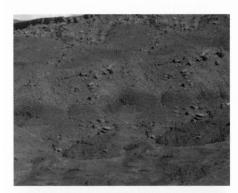

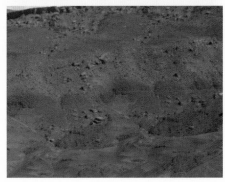

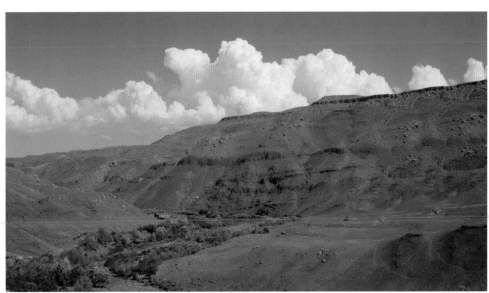

Removing unwanted objects

With lighting, exposure, composition, and timing to manage, the photographer's life can be difficult enough, so few things are more annoying than one unwanted element which ruins an otherwise brilliant picture. Losing that once-in-a-lifetime moment because someone wanders into frame, or missing a classic shot of an ancient monument because one column has been shrouded in scaffolding used to be a disaster, but not any more. Once again, Photoshop offers a variety of techniques to salvage the image. The choice of which technique to use is dictated by a number of factors, including the size of the offending object, the complexity of the image, and the availability of a suitable area from which to take pixels.

Method 1: **The Patch tool**

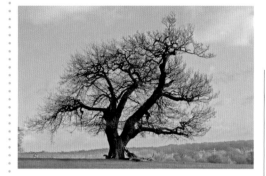

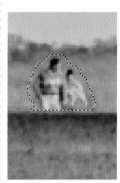

1 The Patch tool provides an excellent method for removing objects from a frame containing different levels of texture, light and shading. The tool automatically matches these elements when it "patches" the new pixels on. Although it works well in most situations by simply copying from one area to another, it can also be used in combination with a layer mask for added control. First, select the Patch tool, then use it to make a selection around the oblivious walkers.

We can't always keep landscape shots free from human interference, and while the couple on the left and the pole and buildings to the right don't completely spoil this image, it would be better with the offending items removed.

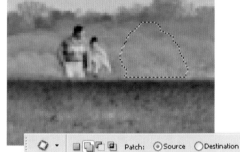

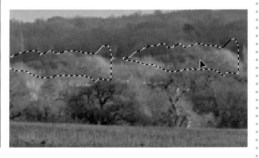

2 Go to the Tool Options bar and select the Source radio button, then drag the selection to an area where you want to copy pixels. In the example, you can see I've done my best to keep the textures lined up in an effort to add to the realism. The Patch tool's live preview makes this easy. You can drag the selection while looking for the best place from which to copy.

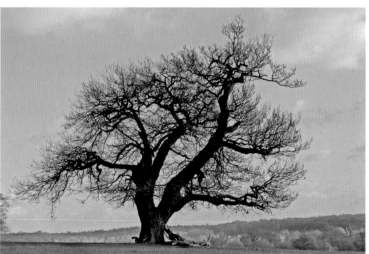

3 Repeat the process with the white pole and the buildings on the other side. As the background is fairly indistinct, you don't need to try too hard to get an effective result.

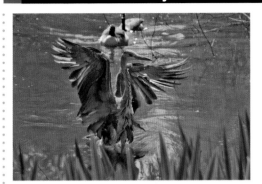

We can use the same basic technique to remove unnecessary detail from the area around this heron.

1 The patching itself is quite simple, but this is a large area to repair, with some wide-ranging differences in light, shade, and texture. This makes it likely that you will have some harsh edges or elements that don't quite line up.

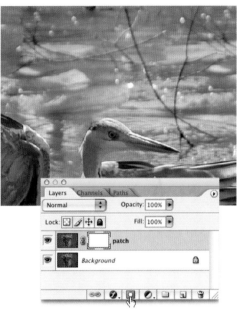

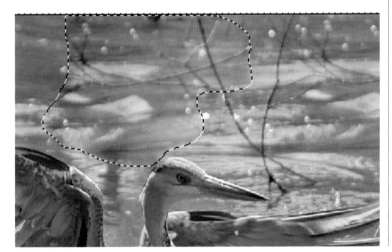

3 Now paint on the mask with a soft-edged, low-opacity brush in black to soften any harsh edges or irregular areas. The final result looks much improved.

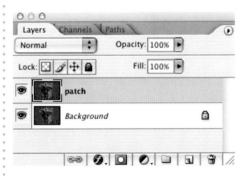

2 Layer masks are key to resolving this. First, undo the patch. Now make a duplicate of the background layer, naming it "patch." Activate this layer, and redo the patch as before.

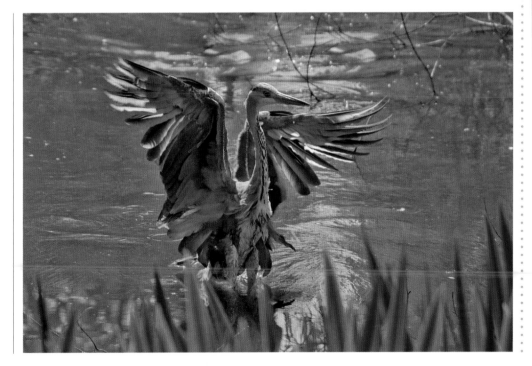

Removing unwanted objects

Method 3: **Copying with clipping masks**

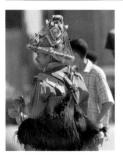

There are times when removing an unwanted element proves to be a real challenge. In the previous examples, we could rely upon a suitably sized area from which to copy pixels. In this image, the people in the background spoil the composition, but the difficulty of removing them is compounded by the lack of a large enough area from which to clone or copy. We could work piecemeal, but that would be laborious, and the potential for a pattern to repeat or multiple seams to appear would be high.

1 The secret in these situations is to look for any area big enough to act as a starting point from which to make a selection to copy. You want something that could be increased in size without looking obvious, and the more uniform, the better. An alternative image could also be used, but sticking with the original means we already have the correct colors, white balance, and tones in place. Here, the area to the top right of the hat looks a good candidate.

2 First make a selection of the area to be removed. I've also included the unidentifiable blue object which is equally distracting. Fill the selection with a white, then deselect.

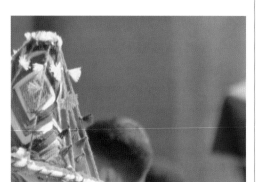

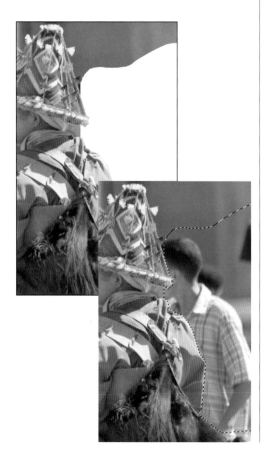

3 Hide the layer, then make a selection of the sample area that will be used to replace the unwanted elements. With the background layer active, press Ctrl/Cmd + J to copy and paste the selection to a new layer. Name and restack the layers as shown.

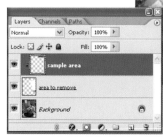

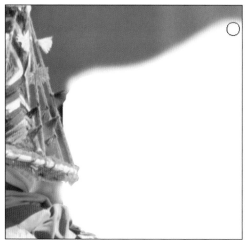

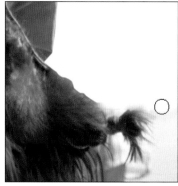

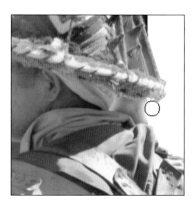

4 Ultimately, we will make a clipping mask between the top two layers, but to help avoid any harsh seams, use a soft-edged brush at 70% opacity and paint with white along the top edge, bottom edge, and left edge just below the hat of the white shape you created in Step 2. This effectively makes a feathered edge in those areas only. For best results, it's important to keep the other edges crisp and sharp.

5 Activate the sample area layer and press Ctrl/Cmd + T to bring up the Free Transform bounding box. Drag the bottom middle handle of the bounding box downward until the pixels completely cover the white area on the layer below. Press Return to confirm the transformation.

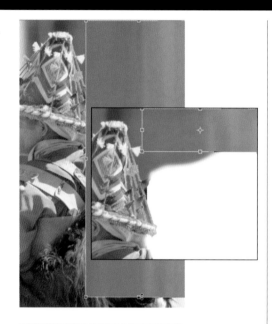

TIP

If there are any visible seams, it will be as a result of the hand painting you did with white to soften the edges. If the line was not soft or subtle enough, the seam may be quite evident.

This is easily dealt with. Add a layer mask to the bottom layer of the clipping mask pair and paint gently on the mask with a soft, low-opacity brush in black and the seams will fade away.

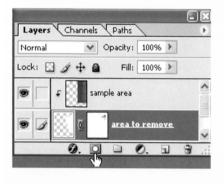

6 Now make a clipping mask between the top two layers. The quickest way to do this is to position the cursor between the two layers in the Layers palette (see example), then hold down the Option/Alt key and click when you see the cursor change to two black circles. Here's the result of the clipping mask.

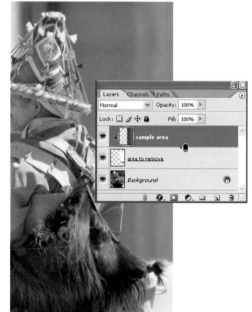

7 The bottom right corner of the image reveals a remnant of the person we have removed. Removing these last traces is simple: use the clone stamp tool as discussed on page 83.

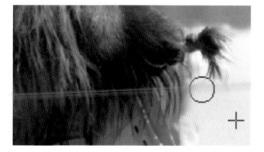

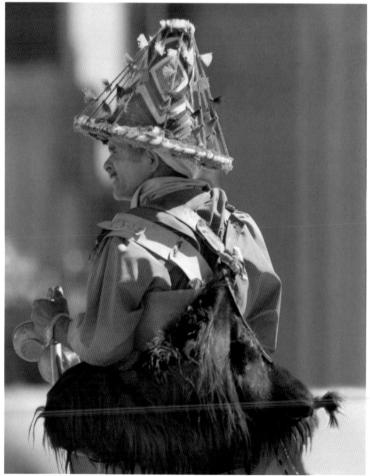

Removing unwanted objects

Method 4: **Airbrush**

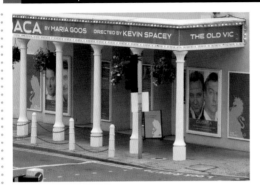

The picture showing the facade of one of London's most famous theaters is spoiled by some unsightly elements that have crept into the picture. These include a traffic stanchion in the bottom left, the wires in the top right corner, and a white sign that obscures one of the pillars. To get rid of these, we'll use some of Photoshop's tricks, plus a tool that harks back to pre-computer days: the airbrush.

1 For accuracy, we start by masking off the areas that need to be protected from our work. The conduit in the top right corner sits on a flat uniformly colored wall. This is a perfect environment for the airbrush. Make a selection as shown.

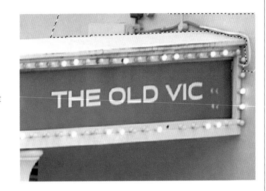

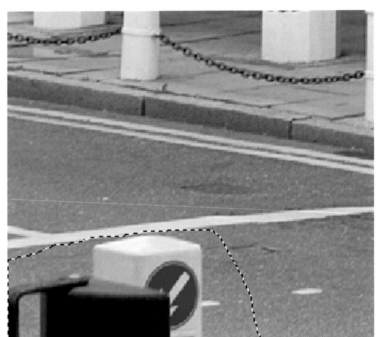

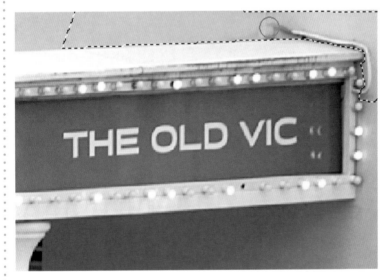

2 Use the eyedropper to sample a color from within the selected area, then paint on a new layer within the selection using a large soft edged airbrush at low opacity. It is best to build up the paint gradually for a more realistic effect.

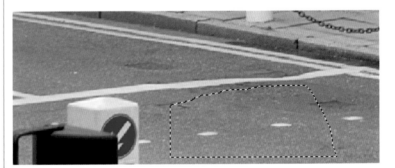

3 Next we'll deal with the traffic stanchion in the bottom left corner. The first thing to note is the uniformity of the surface of the road—we can use this to our advantage. Make a feathered selection a little larger than the area to be removed, then drag the selection to an area from where we can copy pixels.

4 Hold down the Ctrl/Cmd + Alt keys and drag the selection back over the stanchion, positioning it so that the white lines line up. This action has made a floating selection.

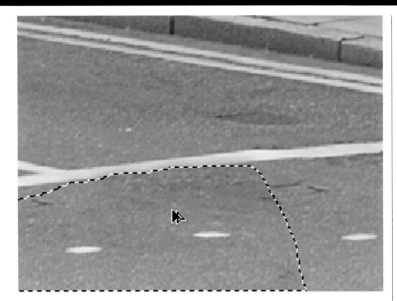

5 With the selection in position, press Ctrl/Cmd + D to deselect. This flattens it back into the layer. Your success will depend on the location of the selection, but if you see any seams try the process again, looking for areas of similar tone and shade from which to copy.

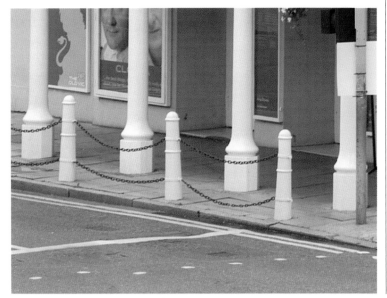

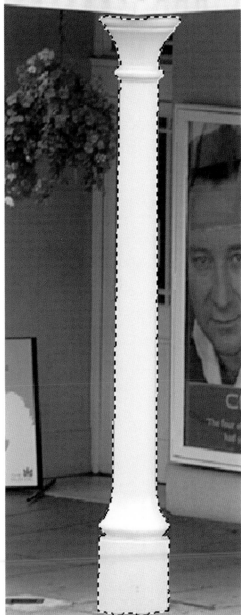

6 We could use a similar technique to hide the traffic light obscuring the pillar. This time, much of the work has been done for us as we have an identical perfectly positioned unblemished pillar just waiting to be used. Even the selection is easy. The Magic Wand tool makes light work of it.

Removing unwanted objects

Airbrush continued

7 With the background layer active press Ctrl/Cmd + J to make a duplicate layer and drag the pillar into place, scaling it as necessary so it completely hides the original pillar.

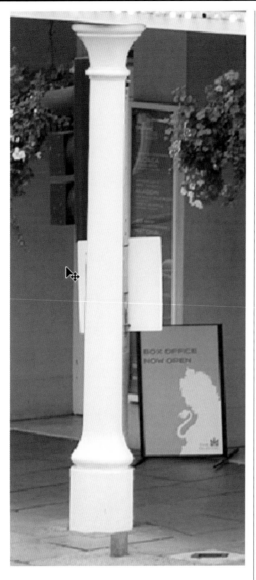

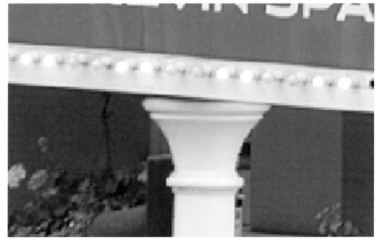

8 The top right corner of the pillar needs to be hidden under the roof. Add a layer mask to the pillar layer and paint on the mask with black paint to hide the corner.

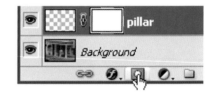

9 We are now left with traffic lights that seem to be growing out of the pillar. Here the hanging flower basket comes to our rescue, along with another old Photoshop favorite: the Clone Stamp. Create a new layer for the cloned flowers. This makes it easy to edit if you're not happy with the result and need to start again or fine tune your work. The new layer should sit between the background and pillar layers.

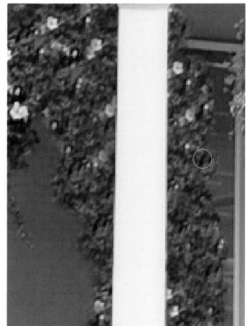

10 Select the clone stamp tool, then go to the Tool Options bar and ensure the "Use all layers" check box is enabled. Press Alt/Option and click the area from which you want to start copying pixels. Now clone onto the new layer until the traffic light, gray post and white sign are covered.

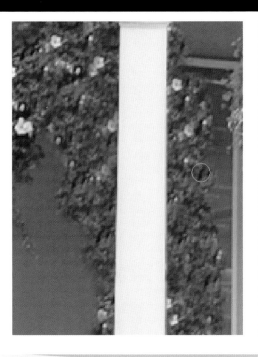

11 Repeat this process at the base of the pillar where a small area of the traffic light post is exposed. One large stroke should be sufficient to remove the post, however working on a separate layer again gives you the freedom to perfect your attempts.

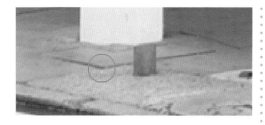

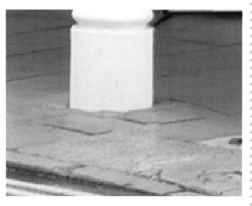

12 The end result is a clean image devoid of any distracting or unsightly objects, and all engineered with the minimum of effort.

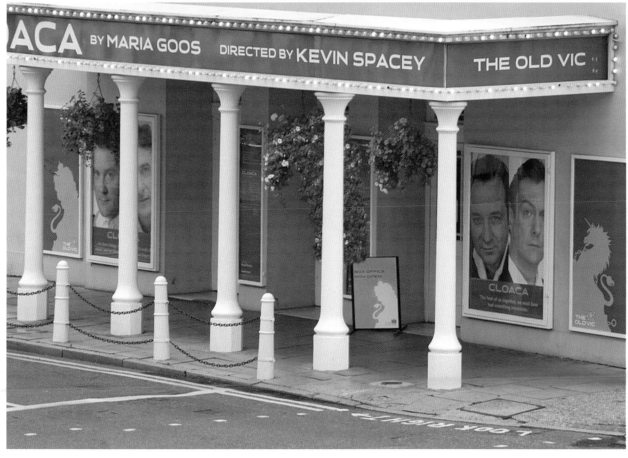

Correcting perspective

If you still have recurring nightmares from school art classes where you had to draw lines and vanishing points to create perspective guides, this is where you get your revenge. As vital as perspective is to creating realistic artwork, it's not always so desirable in photographic composition. Thankfully, Photoshop makes light work of removing its ill effects, without a manually calculated vanishing point in sight.

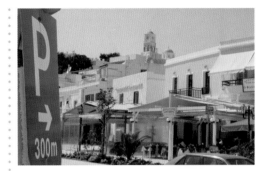

Before correcting perspective, we need to determine the kind of correction required. The parking sign in this first image is the element requiring correction. The camera lens was almost level with the bottom of the sign, so a little distortion is visible on the bottom edge. The top of the sign was considerably higher than the lens, which accounts for its exaggerated distortion.

1 In this case, only one side needs correction, so we'll use the Free Transform tool. First make a selection of the sign. Go to Edit > Transform > **Free Transform** or press Ctrl/Cmd + T. You should see a bounding box around the selection.

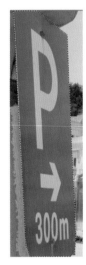 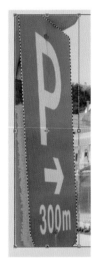

2 Press and hold the Ctrl/ Cmd key, then position the cursor over the top right anchor point of the bounding box. Drag upwards, while keeping the Shift key pressed. The Shift key constrains the movement as you drag, which stops you drifting away from the vertical axis. Drag to the top of the image area as shown. Press Return to confirm the transformation.

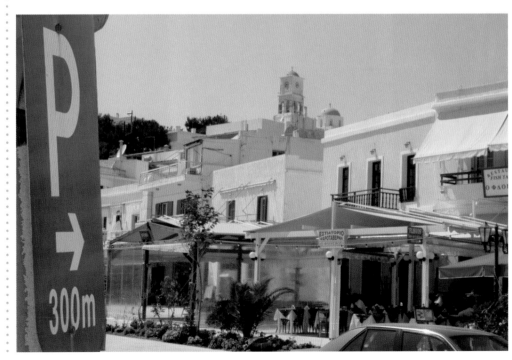

84

Symmetrical correction

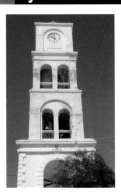

A more typical perspective correction task involves making adjustments symmetrically. The photograph of the white stone tower was taken from a low angle, resulting in equal distortion to both sides of the tower. Photoshop's answer to this common problem is the Perspective tool.

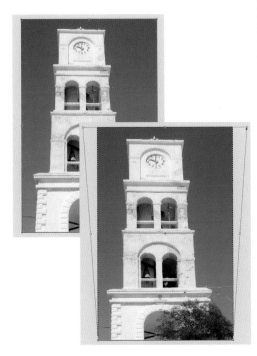

1 Press Ctrl/Cmd + A to select the whole image, then go to **Edit > Transform > Perspective** to reveal the Perspective tool's bounding box handles. Drag the top right corner handle to the right until you have corrected the distortion. You can do this by eye, which works well in this situation. Alternatively you can use a guide positioned on a known rectangular object—such as a door—to match the sides.

2 One consequence of large adjustments is the disproportionate scaling of the image. The adjusted image now looks squat. To remedy this, drag the bottom left and right handles down until the effect is removed. Be careful not to chop the top of the tower off while doing this.

Correction with the Crop tool

The Crop tool can also be used to correct perspective. We'll use it here to change the camera position, so it will appear as if the photograph was taken from a position much closer to the foot of the tower.

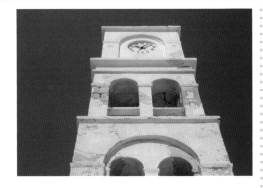

1 Drag out two vertical guides and position them at the left and right edges of the top of the tower. Next, select the Crop tool. Drag out a crop selection, starting from the bottom left of the tower to enclose the whole thing. Be sure that the Perspective checkbox is enabled on the Tool Options bar.

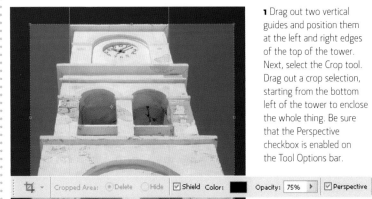

2 Drag the bottom left and right crop handles inwards so they meet with the guides. Holding down the Shift key as you drag will constrain the horizontal movement. Press the Return key to confirm the crop and see the finished result.

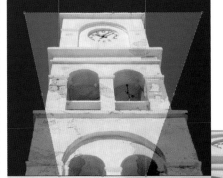

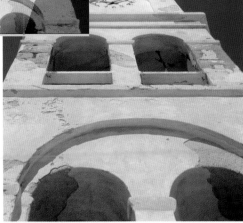

COLOR EFFECTS

Creating black and white from color

Color effects

Tinting images

Emulating photo filters

Creating black and white from color

Black-and-white photography is as powerful today as it was when color photography was just a distant dream. A different set of skills is required when working with black and white, as the absence of color means the interplay of shape and contrast must work harder to tell the story or set the mood, but when it works, it's very effective.

Some cameras have a dedicated black-and-white mode, but even if yours doesn't, you can still work in black and white. In fact, it often works better to shoot in color and convert later on. Photoshop offers a breathtaking array of techniques for converting color to black and white (or more correctly, grayscale), and these enable you to control the process with a degree of finesse that would be difficult to match in the field.

Method 1: **Desaturation**

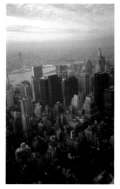

This shot was taken early one winter's morning in New York. The sky had a dramatic quality and there was a fine haze rising to meet the colder air at higher altitudes. The image works well in color, but it also has potential for a striking black-and-white impression of the city.

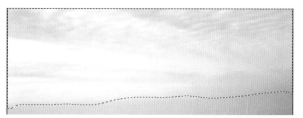

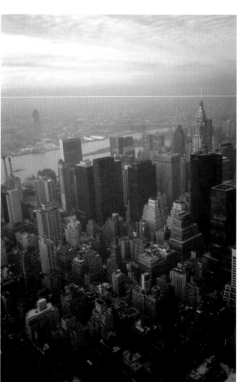

1 The most obvious way of converting color to black and white is to convert the mode to grayscale (**Image > Mode > Grayscale**). This is okay, but there are better alternatives. The first is desaturation—removing the visible color information but maintaining the RGB status of the file. This means that if you wanted to add a tint later you could do so without having to change color mode again. Go to Image > Adjustments > Desaturate (or press Ctrl/Cmd + Shift + U).

2 The problem with desaturation is that it often delivers a flat, uninspiring rendition. We can improve this, however. Analyzing the photo, we need to strengthen the texture in the sky by darkening the shadows and midtones, but the buildings below need a general increase in contrast to remove the haziness. It's best to treat the sky and the buildings as separate entities. Make a feathered selection of the sky, using the natural division of the rising dark haze as a guide.

3 Press Ctrl/Cmd + J to copy and paste the selection to a new layer, and rename it "sky." Add a Levels Adjustment Layer to it, making sure the two layers are combined as a clipping mask. To bring out the sky texture, drag the Black and Gray point markers to the right as shown.

4 Depending on the amount of feathering and the position of your selection, you may see a dividing line after the Levels adjustment has been made. This is easily removed by adding a layer mask to the sky layer (set to Reveal All) and painting on the mask in black until the edge disappears. Work carefully with a soft brush at a low opacity and the result should look something like this.

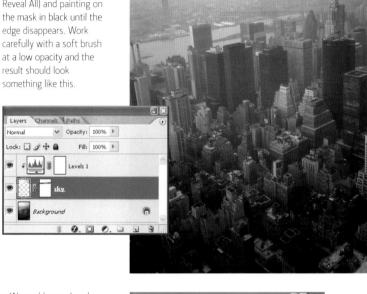

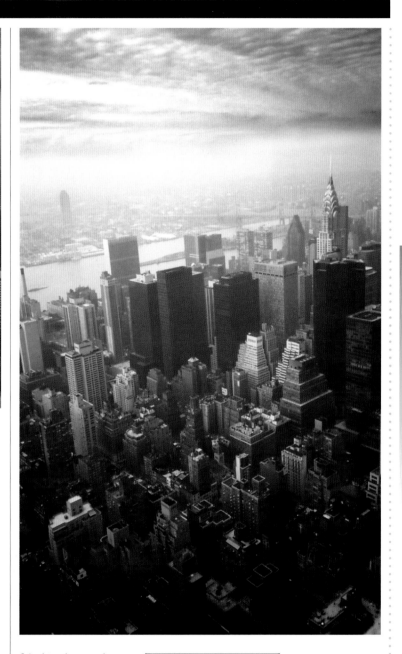

5 We could use a Levels adjustment layer to add contrast to the buildings, but there is an alternative route. Go to **Layer** > **New Adjustment Layer** > **Curves** to add a Curves adjustment layer to the background layer.

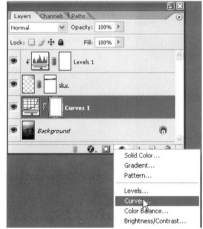

6 Applying the curve shown increases midtone contrast, at slight expense to the highlights and shadows. This diminishes the haziness in the area of the buildings. The final image is far more striking, and much closer to what the photographer originally envisioned.

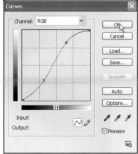

Creating black and white from color

Method 2: **Single Channels**

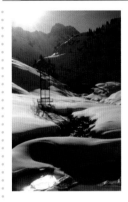

In traditional black-and-white photography, color filters are often used over the lens to create dramatic contrast, the reason being that hues that are quite different in real life can merge into one when seen in grayscale. For instance, a strong blue sky with white clouds can appear weak in a black-and-white photograph. A red filter placed over the lens will darken the blue sky, making the white clouds stand out, because the red filter blocks the blue color waves more effectively than it does colors that are nearer to red. As a result, a red car in the same scene would look lighter. In short, when a color filter is used in black-and-white photography it lightens elements of its own color and darkens elements of its complementary (opposite) color.

We can see this principle in action in Photoshop and use it to create some very different styles of black and white. In this photograph of a mountain stream in the French Alps, the combination of strong contrast and lighting with the sensual curves of the glistening snow makes it an ideal candidate.

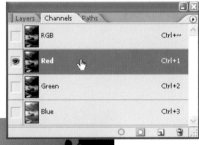

1 Go to the Layers palette, click the Channels tab, then click on the Red channel. The image seen will resemble the result that a red filter over the lens would have generated, with a darkening of the blue-tinted areas that makes for a moody, sophisticated image. For comparison, click on the Green channel. The result is similar to the Red channel but less pronounced. Finally, look at the Blue channel—it's lighter, since most of the image is blue.

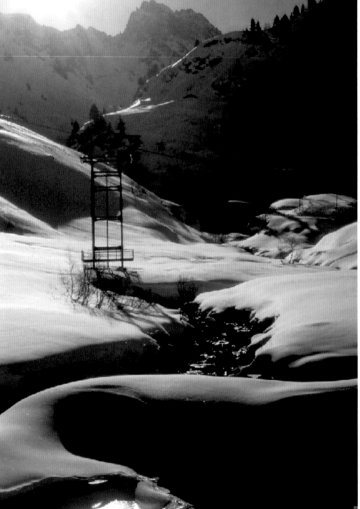

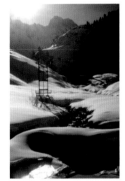

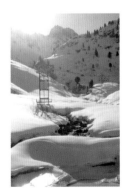

2 Without doing any work, we have three different ready-made black-and-white effects. All we have to do is choose our preferred option: dark and moody. Click on the Red channel. The following keyboard shortcut sequence makes light work of turning it into a new document:

- Ctrl/Cmd + A (selects all)
- Ctrl/Cmd + C (copies the selection to the clipboard)
- Ctrl/Cmd + N (creates a new document of the same proportions as whatever we have on the clipboard. The document will also be a grayscale as we only have one channel selected)
- Enter/Return (to confirm the settings. No changes are necessary)
- Ctrl/Cmd + V (to paste the contents of the clipboard to a new layer)

That's all there is to it. Use Levels and Curves if you want to fine-tune the result.

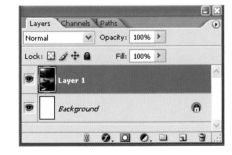

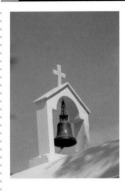

Using the channels straight out of the box works brilliantly, as long as one of the channels gives you the desired result. If not, some manual mixing is the best solution. The Calculations command is your best resort—don't let the name put you off, as no math on your part is required. This image of the bell and cross is our next challenge.

1 Checking the channels shows that the Red channel offers the best contrast between the sky and white cross. However it's not very strong and the range of tones isn't varied enough to create a strong result.

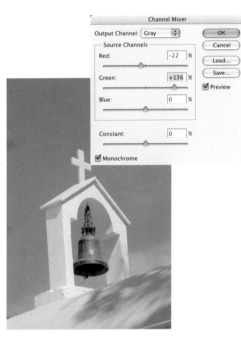

2 Keep the Red channel active and go to **Image > Calculations**. Because the Red channel was active, the Red channel appears in the Calculations dialog box. Source 1 and 2 are set to the same document, layer, and Red channel, which means they will be combined for the calculation to take place. The blending drop-down is set to Multiply. This works in exactly the same way as the normal layer blend modes. Multiply will darken the image, but based on the red channel. Therefore blue elements or elements with a blue cast will become darker than other elements. Set the Result drop-down box to New Document to create a new multichannel file based on the calculated result.

3 In this case, multiplying the Red channel works perfectly. The blues are darkened, creating this bold final image.

Staying within the context of mixing and calculating channel values, another powerful option is the aptly named Channel Mixer. This command allows us to mix the values of each of the channels, providing us with an enormous variety of combinations. In this shot there should be no mistaking the flower from the leaves and stem. However, after desaturation the greens and pinks merge.

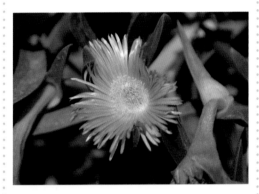

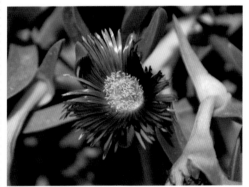

1 Make sure the RGB composite channel is active, then go to **Image > Adjustments > Channel Mixer**. Enable the Monochrome checkbox. Changing the percentage values for each of the Red, Green, and Blue channels will dramatically influence the image. Traditional black-and-white photographers might consider using a green color filter here, as this will lighten the greens of the foliage and darken the pink flower (pink is almost complementary to green). To emulate this in the Channel Mixer, change the values by boosting green and diminishing red.

2 The result is very different from the original desaturated version. We can use the idea of a color filter as a guiding principle here, or just adjust the settings by eye. The main thing to keep in mind is that the total percentage value of all channels combined should be roughly around 100% with a variance of 20% or so. Your eyes will tell you this as you experiment—any extreme value above or below 100% simply won't look good.

ANOTHER OPTION

For a slightly less dramatic result, try combining the Red and Green channels, again using the Multiply blend mode. The difference is subtle, but it demonstrates the fine control you have using this technique.

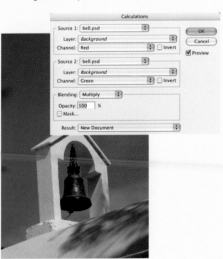

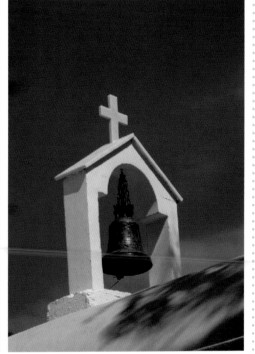

Color effects

Photoshop is a potent color adjustment tool, but there are times when we want to go beyond correcting colors, to changing them altogether. Transforming a yellow rose to a red one, or a pink dress to a more conservative blue one can make an enormous difference to advertisers or art directors. Doing so takes work to get realistic results, but there are several ways to tackle it.

Method 1: **Replace Color**

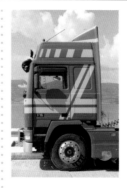

The first method is the Replace Color command—an all-in-one tool that enables us to make a selection, then change the Hue, Saturation, and Lightness from within one dialog box. In this example, Replace Color makes it easy to change the color of the yellow stripes on this truck.

1 Make a rough selection around the lorry. The purpose of this selection is to define the area within which the tool will operate. The actual pixels to be changed will be defined in the next step.

2 Go to **Image** > **Adjustments** > **Replace Color.** The top half of the dialog box shows a Preview window. Choose the Selection radio button so we can see the selection being made. Using the + Eyedropper, start to build up the selection by clicking and dragging through the various shades of yellow. You can use the Eyedropper either in the image window or the preview window. If you make a mistake and select too much use the - Eyedropper to subtract the unwanted pixels. The Fuzziness slider performs a similar role to the Tolerance setting of the Magic Wand: higher values increase the scope of the tool, lower values limit its range.

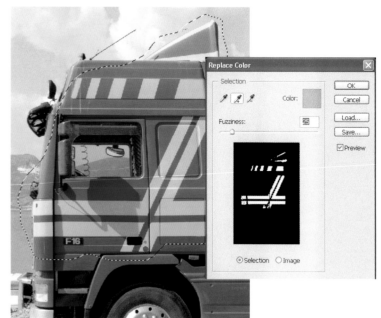

3 With the selection made, it's time for the color change. Use the Hue slider to move upwards and downwards through the different colors until you find a suitable replacement, then use the Saturation slider to increase or decrease the color's strength.

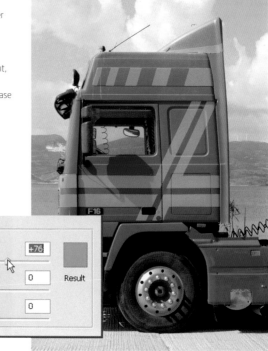

REPLACING WITH LAYER MASKS

Transforming these yellow umbrellas into green umbrellas should be easy using the Replace Color tool, but it's not. Getting a selection of the umbrellas without also selecting some of the poles and some of the surrounding area proves impossible.

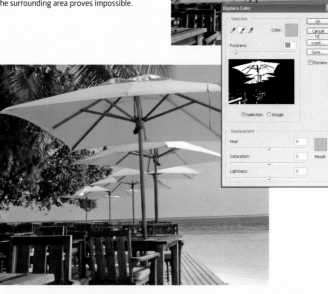

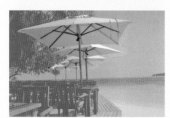

The solution is to make the adjustment to a duplicate later, then add a layer mask, using it to restrict the effects of the Replace Color change to where it's wanted: the umbrellas.

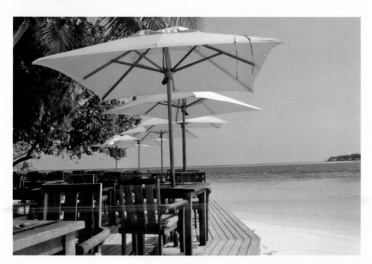

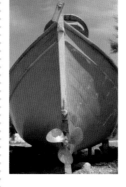

The Hue/Saturation command offers another route to lifelike color change. In this example, we'll use it to change the orange color of the boat.

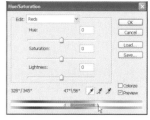

1 Go to **Image > Adjustments > Hue/ Saturation** or press Ctrl/ Cmd + U. The Edit dropdown box displays the range of colors that can be used for the selection. Choosing Master (the default) ensures that all the colors in the image are affected.

2 Now it gets tricky. Orange isn't offered as an option, and the same applies to purple, pink, and a multitude of other mixed colors. However, remember that orange is made up from red and yellow, and all becomes clear. Choose Red as the Edit color and you'll see the range of hues that are controlled by the Red setting at the bottom of the dialog

box. The markers either side of the gray rectangle have a feathering effect on the color selection, so choosing Red actually chooses a range of colors from magenta on the left, to orange on the right. To manually increase or decrease this range of hues, drag the markers or stretch and compress the gray rectangle by dragging its left or right edges.

3 Drag the Hue slider to change the color of the boat, and use the Saturation slider to strengthen or weaken the color. Changing color in this way maintains the photographic authenticity of the image. The luminosity (or brightness information) is preserved, so the worn texture of the old paintwork still shows through.

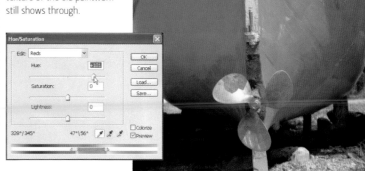

93

Tinting images

Applying a color tint can add a degree of sophistication to an image in the same way as a black-and-white conversion. The color tint unifies the image and can create a theme in a group of related images, or add a new atmosphere to a single shot.

COLOR WASH

The Hue/Saturation command is as adept at tinting as it is at changing specific colors. We'll use it to apply a uniform color wash over this image of a tower.

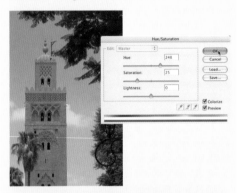

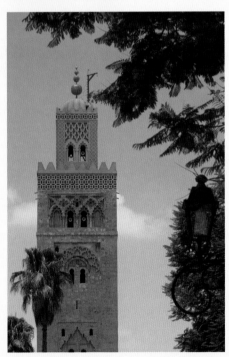

Press Ctrl/Cmd + U for Hue/Saturation. Enable the Colorize checkbox and use the Hue slider to choose the color. With Colorize checked the color used has a global effect, and works as a tint across the image.

Quick-and-dirty sepia tint

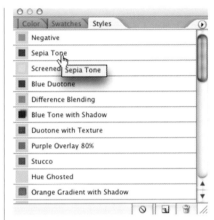

For that authentic, nostalgic, pseudo-vintage look, one tint—sepia—stands above all others. You could use the previous technique to achieve a sepia tint, but there are alternative methods that create a richer tone.

One of those methods is completely automated, which is ideal when you're short on time or low on patience. Here, the timeless quality of the eternal desert makes a perfect subject.

1 If the Styles palette is not open, go to **Window > Styles** to open it. If you don't see the Sepia Tone option in the palette, click the popout button in the top right corner and choose Photographic Effects. Styles don't work on a background layer, so double-click on it and rename it before attempting to use a style.

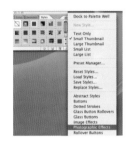

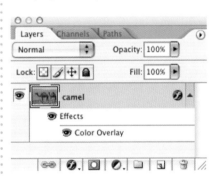

2 Click the Sepia Tone option in the Styles palette to apply it to the layer. The Layers palette reveals how its done. It's nothing more than a single color applied to the layer with a Color blend mode. The same affect could be achieved by creating a layer above the camels, filling it with a brown color, and changing its blend mode to Color.

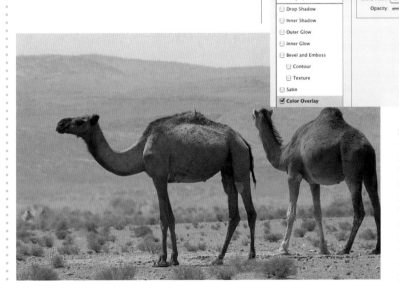

3 If you want to change the color used, double-click either the Effects or the Color Overlay layers to open the Layer Style dialog. From here you can change the color, the blend mode and the opacity. Although this photograph was taken quite recently, it looks as if it could have been exposed 70 years ago.

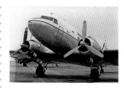

The downside of any automated feature is that the effects produced aren't always as good or as believable as those you might create yourself. Even if the effect works, you may want to fine-tune it to your personal preference. The Color Balance command gives you almost infinite control over the tint effect, as work on this contemporary photograph of a 60-year-old aircraft will demonstrate.

1 First we need a grayscale image to work on. Go to **Image > Adjustments > Desaturate** or press Ctrl/Cmd + Shift + U. Don't convert to Grayscale, as Color Balance won't work in this mode.

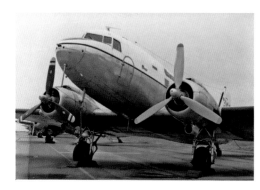

2 Press Ctrl/Cmd + B to bring up the Color Balance command (**Image > Adjustments > Color Balance**). Keep the Midtones radio button selected. This will cause the color effect to impact most heavily on the midtones of the image. Drag the Yellow/Blue slider towards Yellow to emphasise that color. To warm up the sepia, drag the Cyan/Red slider towards Red.

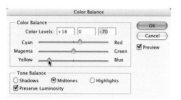

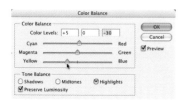

3 For a more antique effect, click the Highlights radio button and make smaller adjustments towards Yellow and Red. This final result looks great, but by experimenting you can achieve a wealth of different looks.

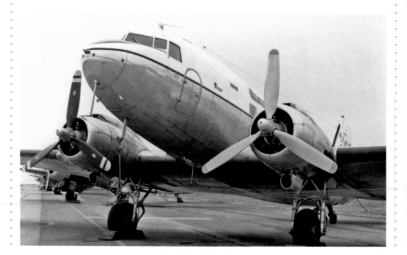

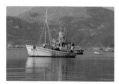

Using a duotone is a popular technique in printed commercial literature. A duotone is a grayscale image where a second color is added to create a richer tone. There are also three-ink (tritones) and four-ink (quadtones) variations. The additional ink(s) extend the tonal range of a grayscale image by mapping different percentages of each ink to different ranges of gray, and the results can be richer, warmer, or colder depending on the inks used. Without access to professional printing services it's difficult to achieve the same effect, but we can approach it using a Gradient Map. We'll apply this treatment to a shot of fishing boats. The gradient map uses preset colors as gradients, but you can mix your own gradient or use the foreground and background colors.

1 Go to **Image > Adjustments > Gradient Map**. Click the arrow next to the Gradient preview to choose a new gradient. Note that the drop-down offers a popout menu if you want to examine other options.

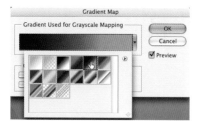

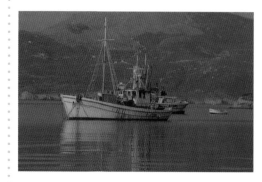

2 By default, the shadows in the image are mapped to the left gradient color, the highlights map to the right gradient color, and the midtones map to the range of tones in between.

BASIC TRITONES

This example shows a three color gradient using blue, red, and yellow from left to right. In this instance, the blue maps to shadows and the yellow maps to highlights, as in the previous step, but now the middle color—red—maps to the image midtones. It's an interesting effect, but is perhaps best saved for the special effects gallery.

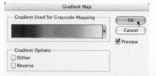

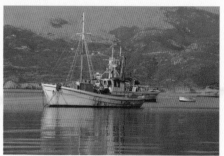

95

Emulating photo filters

In traditional photography, one method of controlling color is through the use of filters, attached in front of the lens to adjust for differences in light or to add tone or color to an image. These filters can be broadly split into two groups: those used for creative purposes or special effects, and those with a more functional purpose (though there is some blurring between these boundaries). To some extent, Photoshop obviates the need for such filters, though there are a few exceptions—polarizing filters, neutral density filters, and UV filters to name just three. But while Photoshop has sealed the fate of the great mass of filters, it also gives us the tools to recreate their effects.

The Graduated filter

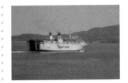

This filter enjoyed its heyday in the 1970s and '80s, when it was used to make a dull sky more interesting, or add an artistic touch to the scene. Strangely, while the effect rarely fooled anyone, it still had an undeniable aesthetic appeal. We'll see if the magic still works on this uninspiring shot.

1 Create a new layer and call it "Gradient." Click on the foreground color, and use the color picker to choose a new color for the sky. Sunset colors are traditionally the most popular, but you can experiment with other options too.

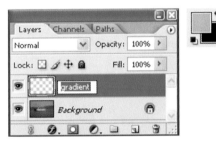

2 Now choose the Gradient tool and select the Foreground to Transparent linear gradient from the Tool Options bar at the top of the screen. Now, with the Gradient layer active, drag the gradient from the top to a point halfway down the image.

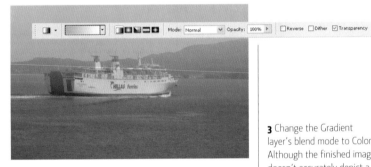

3 Change the Gradient layer's blend mode to Color. Although the finished image doesn't accurately depict a setting sun, it does have a nice retro feel about it.

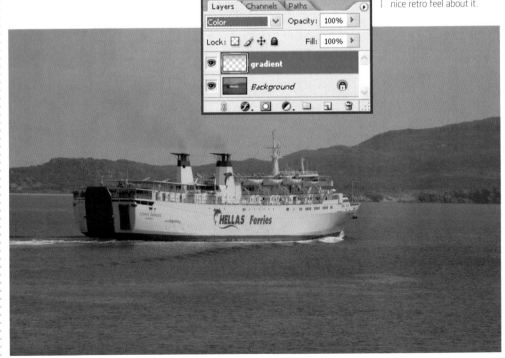

96

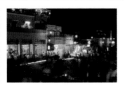

It would be inconceivable to write a piece on traditional photographic filters and not include the starburst filter. The effect became kitsch with overuse, but, used with discretion, it remains an essential element in commercial photography. It's easy to replicate in Photoshop. This slow nighttime exposure, taken in a busy square in Marrakech, provides the perfect backdrop for starbursts, with a dark background and plenty of light.

1 First set the color for the starbursts. Choose the eyedropper tool, then click on one of the lights to sample the color.

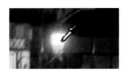

2 Click on the paintbrush tool, then open the brush palette (**Window > Brushes**, if the palette is not already open). Click the popout menu button in the top right corner of the palette and choose the Assorted Brushes set. In this brush set you will find two brushes called Starburst, one small and one big. Click on either of them.

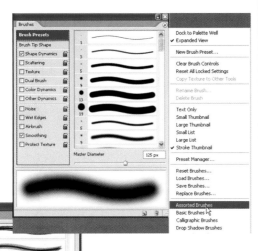

3 A quick way to set the size of the brush is to press the square bracket keys. Click] to increase the size and [to decrease. Size increments are in 10 pixels until you go below 10, when it becomes 1 pixel. Set the brush to 50% opacity.

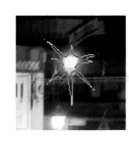

4 Create a new layer then click to make a starburst. If you use the Airbrush option just keep the mouse button pressed and paint will continue to flow. However you may find you get more pleasing results using the brush without Airbrush turned on. You can click multiple times, gauging the effect as it builds.

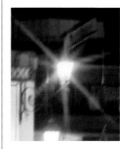

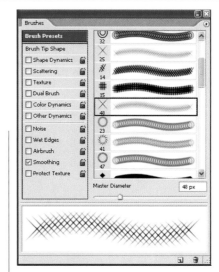

5 For a little variety, we can apply a different style of starburst. In the same palette you will find another brush in various sizes, deceptively named Crosshatch. Ignore the name, as it makes an excellent starburst. Set the size of the brush with the square bracket keys again, and this time click two or three times, each time shifting the mouse a few pixels. This is how a starburst typically appears when reflecting from a complex light with a number of different surfaces.

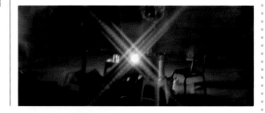

6 Repeat the process, changing the size of the brush for different lights. If you need to match the color of a different light source, Alt/Opt-click on it to sample the color. The hardest thing is knowing when to stop (fewer starbursts works better than more).

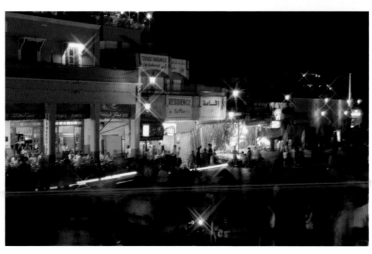

97

Emulating photo filters

COLOR FILTERS

Photographic filters are used with film cameras to intentionally warm up cool colors or cool down warm colors. For example, a magazine advertisement for a mountain lodge hotel may feature the lobby with a log fire. The color of the image may be adjusted to achieve a warm, cozy look. Sometimes the reasons are corrective. A blue 80A filter could be used with daylight film when shooting under tungsten light to prevent an orange cast, or an orange 85B filter might be used when using tungsten-balanced film under daylight.

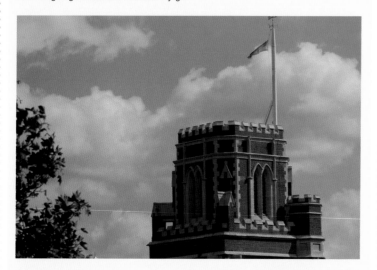

In digital photography, balanced film isn't an issue, but there are still white-balance settings to contend with. An image taken in daylight with the white balance set to tungsten would render a blue cast, as demonstrated here.

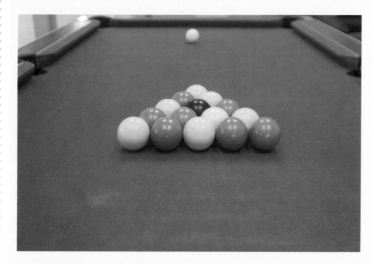

If you take an photograph under tungsten light with the white balance set to daylight, you will see an orange cast.

Such problems have traditionally been rectified in Photoshop using Levels, Curves, and Color Balance (see page 26-29 for details). However, in Photoshop CS, a dedicated command has been added—Photo Filter—which is designed to work in the same way as its real-world counterparts. The only difference is that the filter is used after the image has been taken.

Using Photo Filter for adjustment

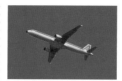

The image of the aircraft was taken with the white balance setting on Tungsten. We'll use one of the photo filters to try to correct the blue cast.

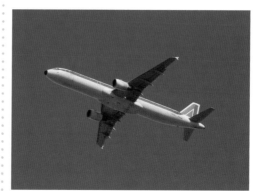

1 Go to Image > Adjustments > Photo Filter. Choose the Filter radio button and select Warming Filter (85) from the drop-down box. The density is set to 25% by default, but we need to increase this to 45% to counter the blue cast. With the Preview check box enabled, you can see the results as adjustments are made. The filter warms up the image significantly.

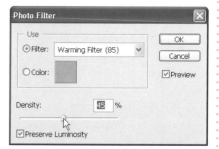

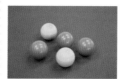 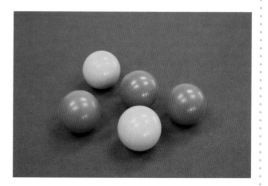

2 The pool ball image needs cooling down to compensate for the orange/yellow cast. Bring up the Photo Filter dialog box again and choose Cooling Filter (82) from the drop-down box. Increase the density to about 32%. The cyan of the filter counters the yellow/orange cast, and the image looks correctly exposed.

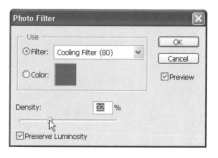

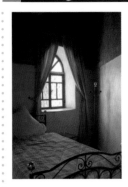

Of course, photo filters are not used solely for correction purposes. They also play a valuable role in creating emotion or a certain ambience. The stone walls of this traditional North African bedroom generate a cold, unwelcome feeling.

1 We can change this mood using a custom color filter, applied as an adjustment layer so changes can be made at a later time. Apply the adjustment layer by clicking the icon at the bottom of the Layers palette and selecting Photo Filter, or choosing **Layers > New Adjustment Layer > Photo Filter.**

2 This time, click on the Color radio button, then click the square color box next to it to open the Color Picker. Use the following RGB color: R231, G152, B9, and set the density to 88%.

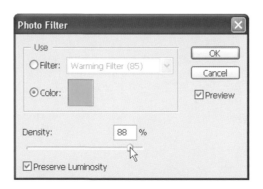

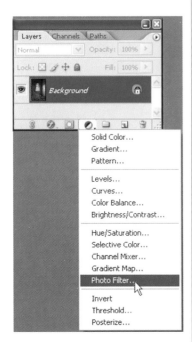

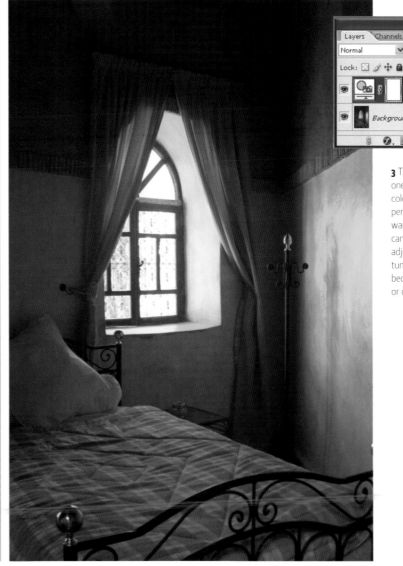

99

3 The result is stronger than one might want for accurate color correction, but it's perfect for generating a warm, inviting light. You can always select the adjustment layer and fine-tune the effect, making the bedroom even more toasty, or cooling it down again.

LIGHTING EFFECTS

Lighting Effects filter

The Lighting Effects Filter is a multi-faceted filter with a huge variety of uses. It can simulate specific qualities of light; utilize and enhance the existing light in a scene; and, by doing both, it can even simulate the effects of lighting that never existed in the original shot. We'll do all three with this shot of a bedroom illuminated by strong afternoon sunlight. Using the Lighting Effects filter, we can completely transform the scene to one of cool blue moonlight mixed with a localized, warm, incandescent light.

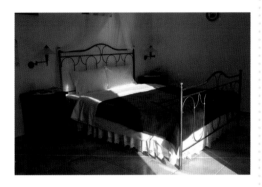

Changing lighting conditions

1 First, duplicate the background layer, renaming the new layer "lighting." Hide the duplicate and activate the original background. Go to **Filter** > **Render** > **Lighting Effects**. Set the Light Type to Spotlight, setting the Intensity about two-thirds of the way towards Full, and the Focus to almost its widest setting. To create a moonlight effect, click the light color square to the right and choose a blue color.

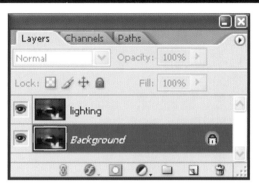

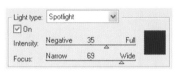

2 The Properties area of the dialog box refers to the materials and surfaces upon which the light is falling, as well as the general ambience and intensity of the light. The settings shown here aim to emphasize the natural light coming in through the out-of-frame French windows, but changing the quality of the light to the blue cast of moonlight.

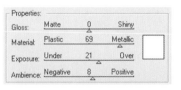

3 In the Preview area, the light can be repositioned using the center handle, or rotated, enlarged, or reduced by dragging any of the four handles on the defining edge of the light. Click OK to confirm the settings.

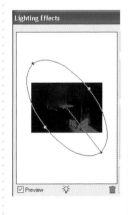

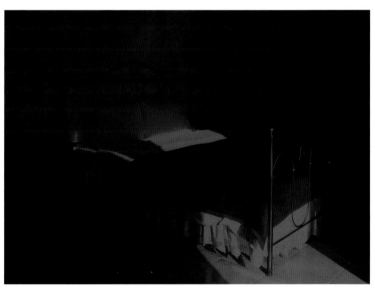

4 Activate the lighting layer and open Lighting Effects again. This time, change the light type to Omni. An omni is a circular light which generates intensity from the center, like a standard domestic bulb. Change the color to a warm yellow.

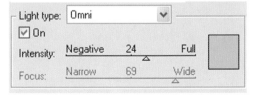

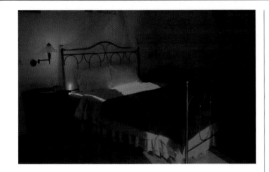

7 By using a layer mask in this way, you are able to exercise far greater control over the exposure and interplay of different lights within a single scene.

8 As a finishing touch, the wall light could use a more obvious light bulb source. Create a new layer at the top of the stack, fill it with black, and change its blend mode to Screen.

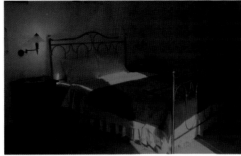

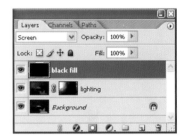

5 Position the light so it sits over the center of one of the wall lights next to the bed. Reduce the size so it only illuminates the immediate area of the wall light. Click OK to fill part of the room with the yellow light.

6 Now we need to combine both versions of the room, so that we see the moonlight and incandescent light simultaneously. Add a layer mask to the lighting layer. Use a soft-edged brush at low opacity and paint on the mask with black, so the bulk of the lighting layer is hidden except for the area around the yellow light.

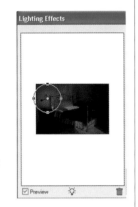

9 Go to **Filter > Render > Lens Flare**. Use the settings as shown. (For a full explanation, see page 106). If necessary, lessen the intensity of the new light by reducing the layer opacity.

ADDING EXTRA LIGHTS

Using the same technique, a whole range of lights could be added, each impacting on its own localized area, without destroying the effects of any other lights in the scene.

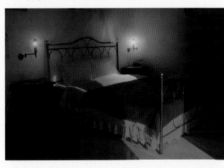

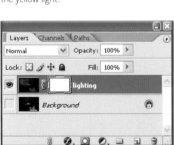

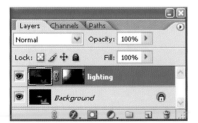

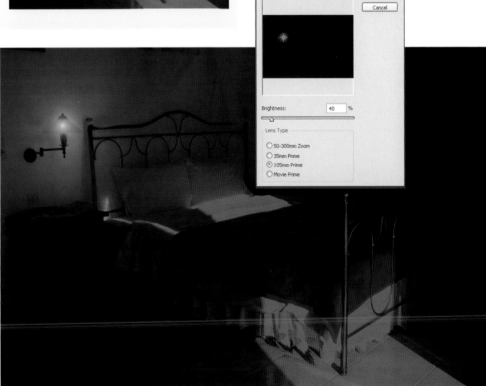

Portrait lighting

LIGHTING EFFECTS

W e can use a similar technique to add mood lighting to portraits. It's possible to create a high-key lighting effect, but in this case we'll take a fairly flatly lit portrait shot and add some more dramatic colored lighting. This technique also simulates a rim-light, used to accent the model from behind.

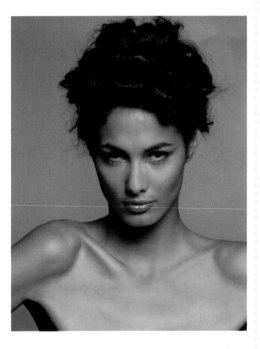

Adding mood lighting

1 First, create two new duplicate layers of the background. Call them "rim" and "fill."

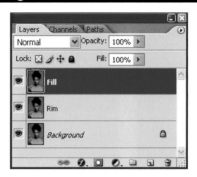

2 Use the Magic Wand tool to create a selection of the background, then invert that selection (Crtl/Cmd + I) to get a selection of the model. Then, create a new layer, and call it "halo." Select this layer, and use the Paintbucket to fill the selection with yellow. Now, with the selection still active, select the background layer and drag it to the Create New Layer icon at the bottom of the Layers palette. Name this layer "model."

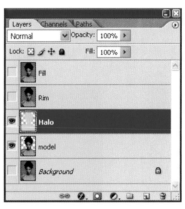

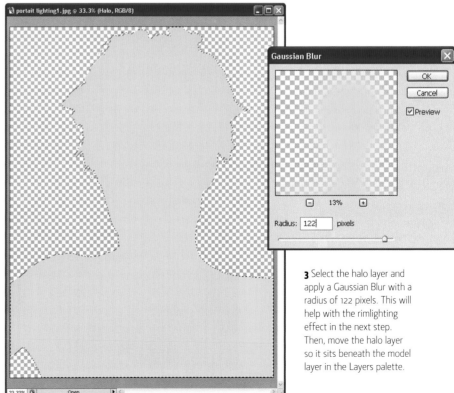

3 Select the halo layer and apply a Gaussian Blur with a radius of 122 pixels. This will help with the rimlighting effect in the next step. Then, move the halo layer so it sits beneath the model layer in the Layers palette.

4 Now for the lighting. Select the rim layer and use **Filter** > **Render** > **Lighting Effects** to create a yellow spotlight, with the settings shown.

5 Select the fill layer and employ Lighting Effects again, this time adding a blue spotlight from the right.

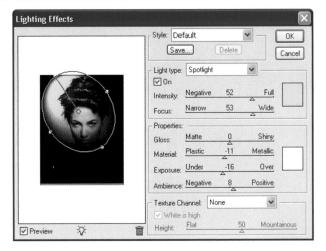

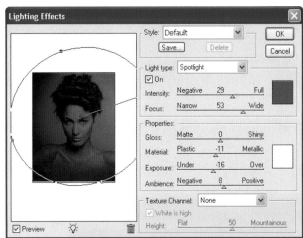

6 The trick here is to vary the blending modes and opacities on the various layers. Select the halo layer and change the blending mode to Soft Light, then go to the rim layer and change the blending mode to Soft Light and the opacity to 80%. Finally, select the fill layer, and change the blend mode to Hard Light and the opacity to 60%.

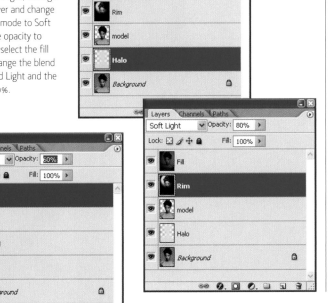

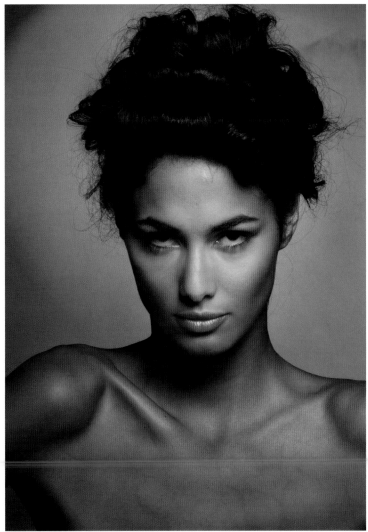

7 To finish the effect, add a layer mask to the rim layer and paint over the face and hair of the model with a large, soft-edged brush. This restricts the effects of the light to the proper areas, and gives you the final, moody image.

Lens Flare

hotoshop's Lens Flare filter is designed to simulate the effect of shining a light into the camera lens, creating the kind of optical effect you might see if you pointed your camera slightly into the sun. The effect has been overused in some quarters but, used creatively to simulate an artificial light source, it can be remarkably photo-realistic.

In the section on creating night shots from day scenes (see page 108), you will see the filter used to good effect to create vehicle headlights, utilizing a method that allows the flare to be movable on the screen. We will take that method a step further here.

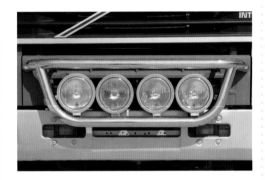

Illuminating headlights

1 To apply the Lens Flare filter to the row of headlights, go to **Filter > Render > Lens Flare**. The dialog box offers four different types of lenses that act as the object refracting the light source. Each lens will refract the light differently, resulting in different types of flare. In addition, the Brightness slider controls the light's strength. To apply the flare, choose a lens type and click or drag in the Preview window to position the light.

2 The light looks effective, but if your aim was a bit off (as mine was), you have no choice but to undo and reapply the effect again, hoping that your aim is better next time. This isn't easy, particularly when the Preview window is quite small. It's not possible to apply the flare to a new layer and position it later, because the filter cannot be applied to a transparent layer. The solution is to apply the filter to a filled layer. Create a new black-filled layer—rename it "new light"—and set the layer blend mode set to Screen.

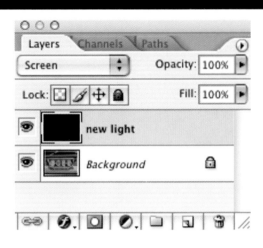

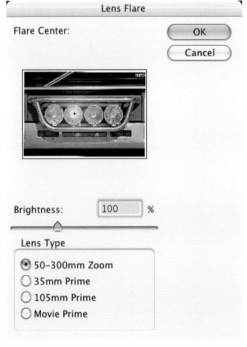

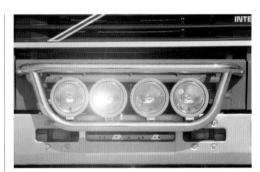

3 Apply the lens flare to the black layer. Don't worry about where you position it. The dark areas of the layer are hidden, as the blend mode is set to screen. This means we can now position the flare anywhere we like. We need to move the flare to the right so it sits over the centre of the headlight, but now we run into a new problem: the left edge of the black layer is now visible.

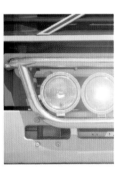

4 This is easily resolved. Double-click the black-filled layer to open the Layer Style dialog box. Make sure you don't click the layer name, as that allows you only to rename the layer. Click to the right of the name. At the bottom of the Layer Style palette, you will see a black slider and a white slider. These allow you to dictate which pixels from the current and visible underlying layers show through, enabling you to remove dark pixels from the current layer or allow bright pixels from lower layers to become visible. It even allows for a range of partially blended pixels to appear with a smooth, graduated finish.

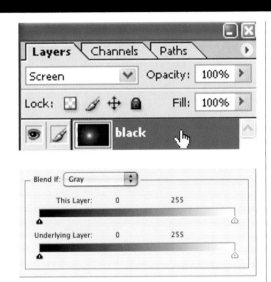

5 Let's put this control through its paces. Choose Gray from the Blend If drop-down. This enables us to set a blending range for all three channels. Alternatively, the Red, Green, or Blue channel can be selected to specify blending just for that channel. The new light layer is the layer that we are interested in, so use the top range of sliders labeled "This Layer." Drag the black slider to the right to about 37. Any pixels with a brightness value of less than 37 (where 0 is black and 255 is white) will now be excluded. By dragging the black slider further to the right, you can increase the range of shades to be dismissed from the final image. Dragging the white slider to the left does the reverse. First the brightest pixels will be excluded, then darker pixels as the slider moves further

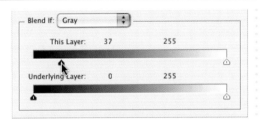

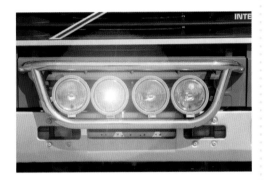

left. This is the result of moving the black slider to 37. In this way, we've removed the vertical line—but only by replacing it with another harsh edge around the lens flare.

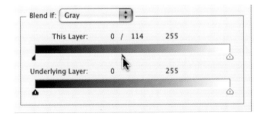

6 Introducing another step will eliminate the hard edge altogether. If you confirmed the last step, press Ctrl/Cmd + Z to undo it and double-click the black layer to return to the Layer Style dialog box. This time, keep the Alt/Opt key pressed and drag the right half of the black slider to the right. Holding down the Alt key splits the sliders into two halves. The result is a partial blend of the range of pixels.

The effect looks the same as when you feather a selection. In the sample image, you will see the numbers 0/114. These define the range of pixels that are being partially blended. The end result is a lens flare that is infinitely editable in terms of its position. We've eliminated any end seams and, by using the sliders in the Layer Style dialog box, we can also control the expanse of flare.

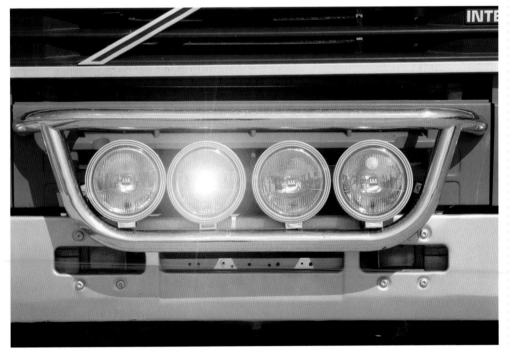

Creating night from day scenes

f you accept that light is one of the basic prerequisites for photography, night photography immediately throws up some daunting challenges. The potential for muddy images devoid of detail and interest is high. As a result, it's tempting to follow the classic Hollywood approach and create night images from daylight scenes. Using Photoshop to do this can add a new dimension to the task, enabling you to decide what kind of night it is (from twilight to the dead of night) and control the ambient light. Here we'll use two different methods that create very different types of night scenes.

Street scene at night

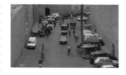

We'll turn this street image into a late evening scene just before full nightfall. First, we'll use a quick and easy method to darken the whole scene.

1 Duplicate the background layer, name the duplicate "night," and change the night layer's blend mode to Multiply. Although we now have a good level of apparent low light, the image still needs darkening. There is also a bit too much color in the scene for the amount of available light. To remedy both points, use a Curves adjustment layer. This will dim the light and provide a slight blue color cast to help the illusion.

Select **Layer > New Adjustment Layer > Curves**, or click the icon at the bottom of the Layers palette while holding down the Alt/Option key as shown. Holding down Alt/Option forces the New Layer dialog box to open. Make sure the checkbox labeled "Use Previous Layer to Create Clipping Mask" is enabled. This means the adjustments we make will only affect the night layer.

2 We'll make three small adjustments. First, darken the whole image by creating the curve In the Composite RGB channel, as shown.

3 To remove some of the color and replace it with a blue night cast, make the next adjustment to the Blue channel. Grab the central point, and drag it upwards slightly to match the curve shown.

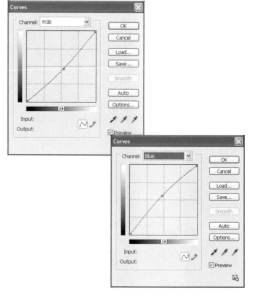

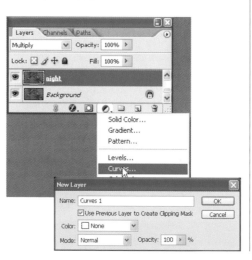

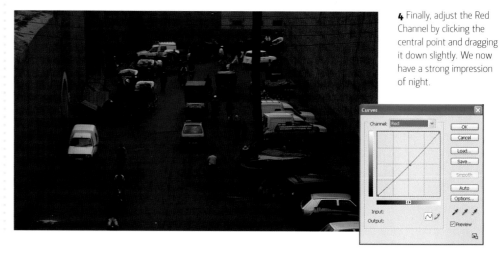

4 Finally, adjust the Red Channel by clicking the central point and dragging it down slightly. We now have a strong impression of night.

108

5 With all of those cars and bikes around, we would expect to see some lights in the scene at this time of night. Switching on the lights will also inject some life into the image. Create a new layer at the top of the Layer stack. Name it "flare," and fill it with black. With this layer active go to **Filter > Render > Lens Flare**. Apply the setting shown.

6 Change the flare layer's blend mode to Screen. This will hide the black area of the layer, revealing only the light.

7 The light now needs to be reduced to the size of a headlight. Press Ctrl/Cmd + T to bring up the Free Transform bounding box. Drag any corner handle towards the center, keeping the Shift key pressed as you drag. Now position the light over the one of the headlights on the white van.

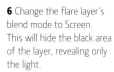

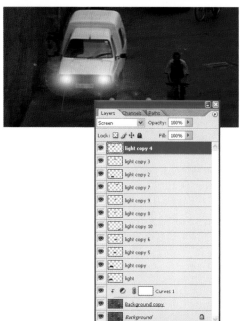

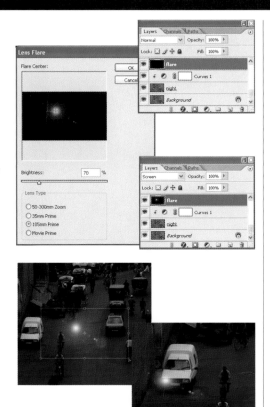

8 To make the second headlight, simply duplicate the light layer. With the Move tool active, keep the Alt/Option key pressed and click and drag anywhere on the light layer. This will duplicate the layer. After duplication, you can position the light in place. Repeat the process to create as many lights as you need. Scaling lights for bikes and vehicles further away adds to the realism.

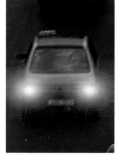

9 Some vehicles are heading away from the camera, which means they should be displaying red brake lights. Place a light over the rear of one of the cars. To turn the light red, go to **Image > Adjustments > Hue/ Saturation**. Enable the Colorize checkbox and drag the Hue slider all the way to create a red tint. Duplicate the light as before.

10 In the final scene, I have added a few more lights, changing the size where appropriate to avoid signs of any obvious duplication. Remember, it's best to duplicate a larger light and scale it down if you want to maintain maximum quality.

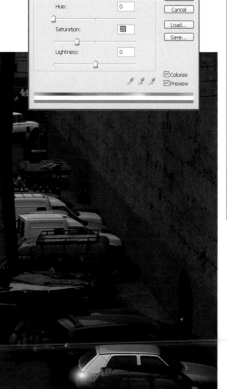

Creating night from day scenes

110

Twilight

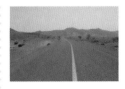

The absence of any sky in the last example meant we had to rely on vehicle lights to add some contrast and lift the image. The next example features a deserted, isolated road without any props that could be used for creating artificial lights. There is a broad expanse of sky, however, and this is perfect for creating an illusion of twilight. This image needs a clear artistic direction if the finished result is not to look weak. One idea is to make it almost abstract, focusing on the strong white center line in the road, leading to the near silhouette of the distant hills. We'll also use a slight variation on the previous method to create a different stage of nightfall.

1 Make a selection of the sky, and create a new layer called "sky."

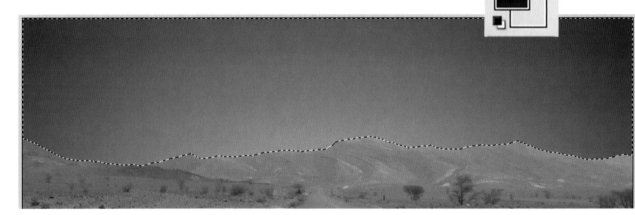

2 Choose a dark and light blue for the foreground and background colors. Make sure the selection is live on the sky layer, then drag a radial gradient, using the foreground to background colors, with the gradient running from bottom to top.

3 As light decreases, our eyes become less able to perceive color, so we'll use a blanket blue wash over the lower part of the scene to mute the color. Duplicate the background layer and name the new layer "blue wash." Press Ctrl/Cmd + U to bring up the Hue/Saturation dialog box. Apply the setting shown to create a blue cast. Make sure the Colorize checkbox is enabled.

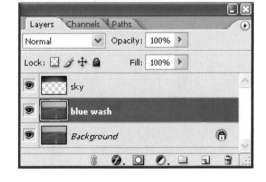

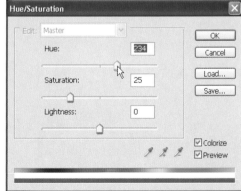

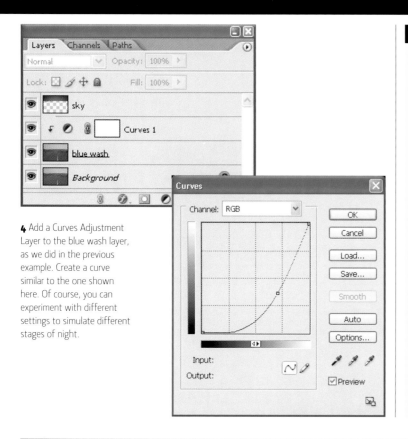

4 Add a Curves Adjustment Layer to the blue wash layer, as we did in the previous example. Create a curve similar to the one shown here. Of course, you can experiment with different settings to simulate different stages of night.

TIP

Turning darkness into dawn is easier than you may think. Add a Hue/Saturation adjustment layer to the top of the layer stack and customize the colors for sunrise. In this case, I added a lens flare to good effect.

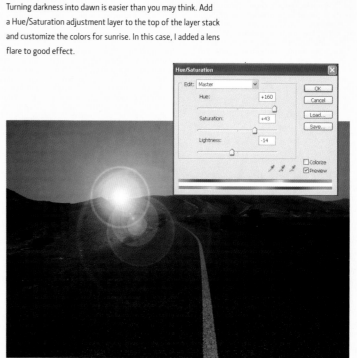

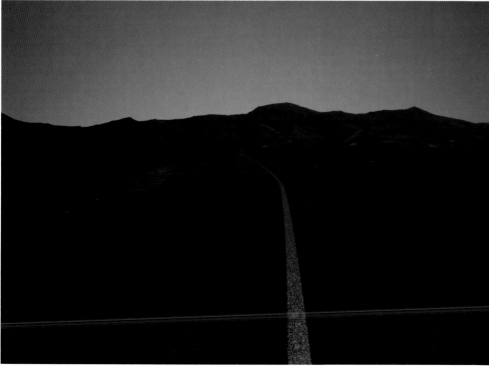

5 In the finished image, I've darkened the scene sufficiently to create an impression of night, while still revealing the white line in the road and some detail in the surrounding areas. You may want to experiment further with different shades for the sky gradient and different degrees of darkness to create a wide variety of night effects.

Creating reflections

Reflections can be a fascinating addition to an image, adding symmetrical forms and an ethereal or painterly quality to an otherwise straightforward shot. It's easy to add a reflection with Photoshop—but there's more to it than simply copying and flipping. To make a realistic impression, a few more tricks are required.

Method 1: **Reflections in water**

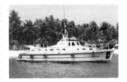

We'll add some reflections to this summer vacation image.

1 Make a selection of the boat. It doesn't have to be too accurate, as we will be applying some distortions later. Press Ctrl/Cmd + J to copy and paste the selection to a new layer. Rename it "boat copy." With the boat copy layer selected, go to **Edit > Transform > Flip**

Vertical to turn the boat upside down. With the Shift key pressed, drag the copied boat downwards until it sits below the original boat. Holding the Shift key constrains the movement as you drag, so that your selection stays in alignment.

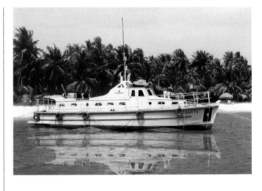

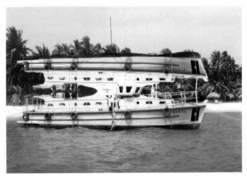

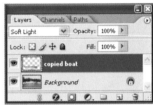

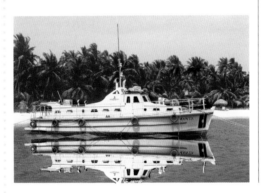

2 Change the boat copy layer's blend mode to Soft Light. Using Soft Light mode allows us to see the texture of the water, but it doesn't break up the image of the boat as a water reflection would in real life.

3 To create the illusion of the reflection breaking up, go to **Filter > Distort > Ripple**. Set the Size to Medium and the Amount to 115%.

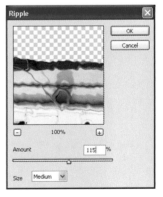

112

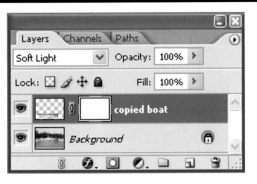

4 We're almost there. The reflection should appear to fade away towards the inverted top of the boat. The problem here is that the whole boat appears at the same intensity. To create a fading effect, add a Layer Mask to the boat copy layer.

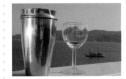

We can use a variation on the same procedure to make a reflection of the cocktail glass in the metal cocktail shaker. The only difference is the kind of distortion we use—a ripple works for water, but in this case it wouldn't be characteristic of the material that is creating the reflection. The next image shows part of the glass copied to a new layer, renamed "glass copy," with the blend mode set to Soft Light, exactly as in the previous example. The selection is left visible to aid clarity.

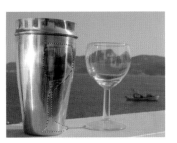

1 Make a selection of the right side of the shaker. Ensure the glass copy layer is selected, then go to **Filter > Distort > Pinch**. Set the Amount to -56%.

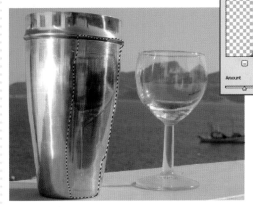

2 The selection around the shaker constrains the effect of the pinch filter. Using a negative value simulates what happens when something is placed close to a circular, reflective object.

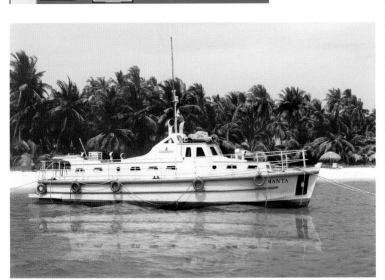

5 Set up the Gradient tool with a black-to-white Linear Gradient. Make sure the mask thumbnail of the layer mask is active, then drag the Gradient from the bottom to about one quarter of the way up the document. If you are not happy with the result, undo (Cmd/Ctrl + Z), then drag it again, until you achieve the right amount of fading.

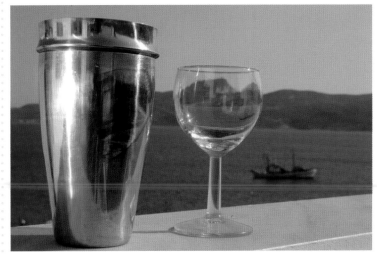

Removing reflections

Removing unwanted reflections works in exactly the same way as removing any unwanted element in an image. The techniques vary in terms of the level of skills required—in this case, a steady hand and a delicate touch.

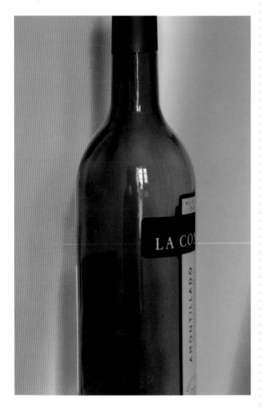

Method 1: **Blur**

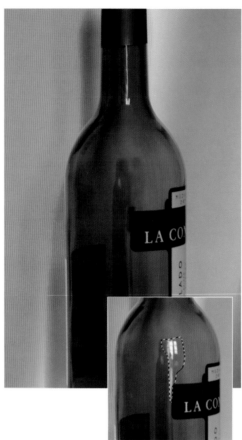

The reflection of the rectangular windows on the bottle is typical of the kind most often requiring removal. If, as in this case, the reflection is white, there is a mostly automated method that works well.

1 Make a small feathered selection of the window reflection and immediate surrounding area. Go to **Filter > Other > Minimum**. Minimum increases the spread of black while shrinking the amount of white. Increase the Radius setting until the desired amount of white area has been removed.

2 Keep the selection live and go to **Filter > Blur > Gaussian Blur**. Set the Radius to around 3.4 pixels, depending on the resolution of the image. The blur will remove any sharp edges that may have appeared from the selection's edge. The end result is the complete removal of the white reflection. Although the minimum filter has also added some darker areas, they are consistent with the patchiness and blended shades of the bottle.

Method 2: **Patch**

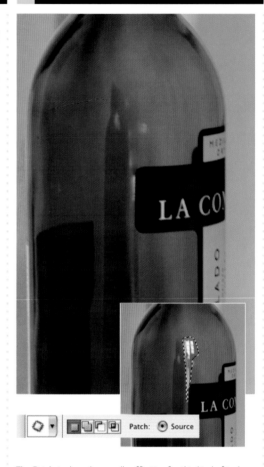

The Patch tool can be equally effective for this kind of task.

1 Select the Patch tool from the Toolbox, and then select the Source option from the Tool Options bar. Create a selection with the Patch tool around the area to be removed, then drag the selection to a suitable area from which to copy.

2 When you've found the right spot, release the mouse button. The obvious reflection has been removed but some streaks of different shades remain, adding to the impression of authenticity.

114

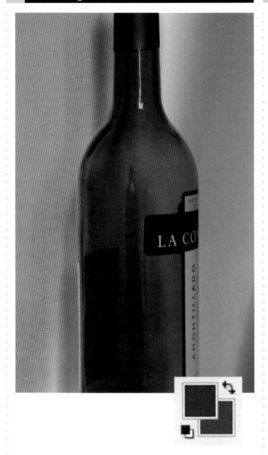

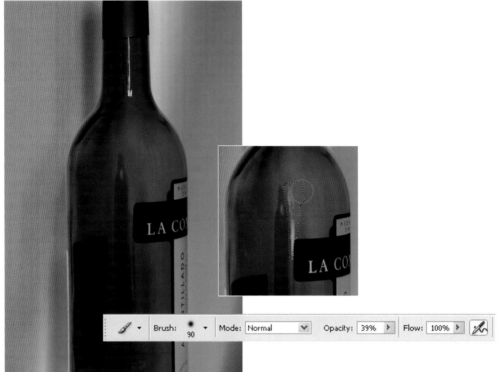

This more traditional method is suitable for those who prefer a manual approach with a bit more room for artistic license.

1 Using the Eyedropper tool, sample two colors from either side of the area to be removed, one for the foreground color and one for the background.

2 Make a selection around the area, then copy it to a new layer (**Layer > New Layer Via Copy**). Drag a Linear Gradient through the selection, using the Foreground to Background colors. The result is smoother than either of the previous techniques.

One final approach is to use the Airbrush. Although many may shy away from this tool in the belief that it demands a high degree of skill, it is worth persevering with, as it offers real control over several techniques, including this one.

1 Once again, use a feathered selection to constrain the spread of paint and sample a color from an area close to where you will be painting. It is best to use a low opacity, soft-edged brush and paint on to a new layer.

2 Gradually build up the layers of paint, resampling new shades often to avoid creating any sharp color transitions. For efficiency, and to avoid breaking the creative flow as you work, use keyboard shortcuts to switch between tools: B for the Brush, I for the Eyedropper.

3 The finished airbrushed result is perhaps the finest and least detectable of all, but it can also be the most time-consuming. The important thing is knowing when to stop. Striving for perfection is all very well, but that last 1% isn't usually worth the effort.

TRADITIONAL DARKROOM TECHNIQUES

Creating film grain

Infrared film effects

Cross-processing

Hand-tinting

Posterization effects

Classic print effects

Solarization

Mezzotints

Reticulation effects

Creating film grain

While film grain can be an unwelcome component of a photograph, when used creatively it almost defines a whole genre of photography. Just as black-and-white photography has become synonymous with tradition, glamour, and sophistication, high-grain images engender a sense of gritty realism. Traditionally, film grain is controlled by many factors, including the emulsion of the film (higher speed films produce coarser grain), exposure settings, and darkroom processes. In digital photography, setting a higher ISO rating on the camera will cause digital noise to appear in a similar way (though the effect is rarely too attractive). As a result, it can be better to recreate the effect using Photoshop's tools.

The choice of image is important—some subjects fit the style more comfortably than others. Black-and-white photography can be very flattering with film grain, as can images with simple or limited tones. Portraits work well, as does anything with a pensive or moody theme. Ultimately you'll know if your choice of image works as soon as you see the effect.

Method 1: **The Film Grain filter**

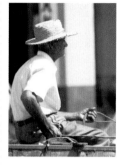

Let's begin with a black-and-white example, and the first of three techniques.

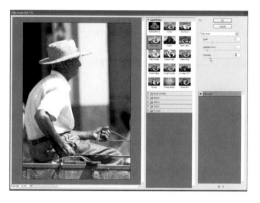

1 Go to **Filter > Artistic > Film Grain**. The filter works by adding a uniform pattern to the shadows and midtones and a smoother pattern with higher saturation to the highlights. Use the Grain slider to define the amount of grain. The Highlight slider increases the amount of highlight in the image. For greater realism, keep the Intensity setting low. The settings shown in the example render a subtle effect. Experiment with the settings so you can see the wide range of possibilities. The more familiar you become with this filter, the more able you will be to fine-tune the effect for your own images.

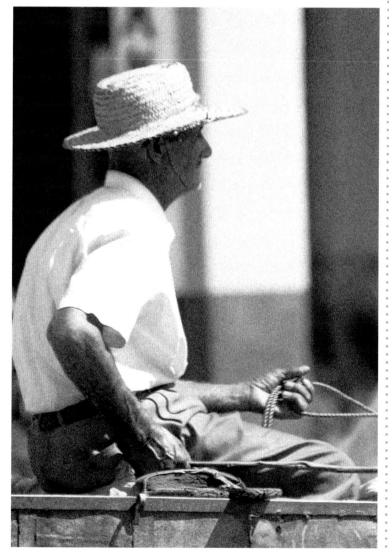

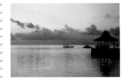

An alternative method is to use the Noise filter. While this filter, like Film Grain, is mostly used to eliminate banding in blended shapes by covering the joins with texture, it's equally adept at producing film grain effects. We'll use a color image this time—albeit one that's almost monochromatic.

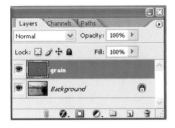

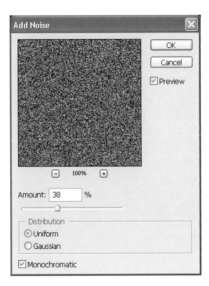

1 Create a new layer named "grain," and fill it with gray (R:122, G:122, B: 122 will work effectively). Activate the new layer, then go to **Filter > Noise > Add Noise**. Set the Distribution to Uniform, check the Monochromatic checkbox, and set the Amount to 38%. Selecting the Gaussian option would create a less subtle effect—the Monochromatic option ensures that only grayscale noise is generated.

If you opt for this method, you can make further adjustments just by changing the blend mode or altering the opacity of the gray layer. For a more pronounced, high-contrast effect, change the blend mode to Overlay . Or, for an even stronger effect, try Vivid Light.

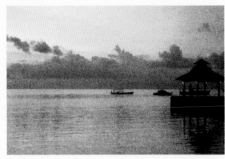

Overlay

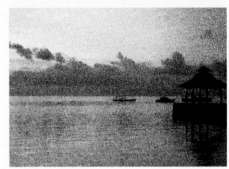

Vivid Light

119

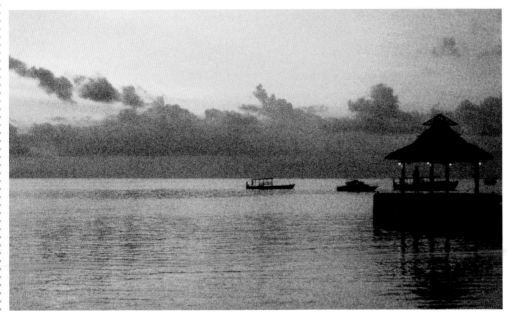

2 Change the grain layer's blend mode to Soft Light. The effect is subtle, with the grain being just discernible.

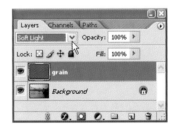

Creating film grain

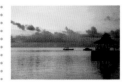

A common characteristic of many images with high grain is a greater profusion of grain in the shadows and midtones, with diminishing or no visible grain in the highlights. We'll recreate this effect on our finished ocean sunset.

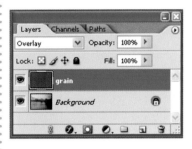

1 If you haven't already done so, change the grain layer's blend mode to Overlay. Now hide the gray layer and activate the background layer.

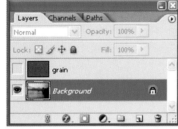

2 To create a Luminosity mask, press Ctrl + Alt +Shift + ~ on your PC (Mac users, press Cmd + Opt + ~). Next, invert the mask (Ctrl/Cmd + Shift + I).

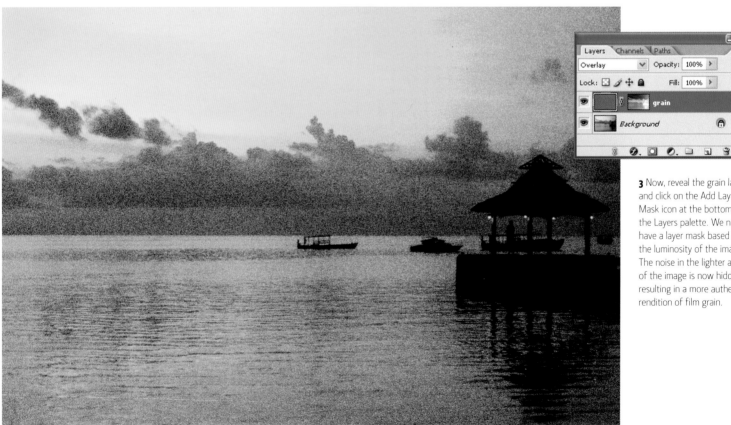

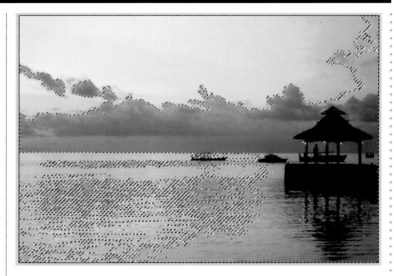

3 Now, reveal the grain layer, and click on the Add Layer Mask icon at the bottom of the Layers palette. We now have a layer mask based on the luminosity of the image. The noise in the lighter areas of the image is now hidden, resulting in a more authentic rendition of film grain.

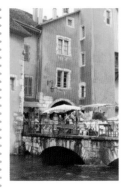

Our next option utilizes Layer Styles. We'll apply it to this shot of an old French market town. Layer styles don't work on background layers, so you first need to rename the background layer, then click on the Layer Style icon at the bottom of the palette and choose Pattern Overlay.

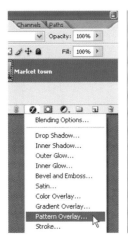

1 Click the little arrow to the right of the thumbnail image shown in the dialog box to reveal a palette of patterns. Click on the arrow to the right of the palette to reveal a drop-down list. Choose Texture Fill from the list (it's near the bottom). When the new pattern set loads, hover your cursor over the thumbnails to see the names of the different textures. Choose the one called "Burlap."

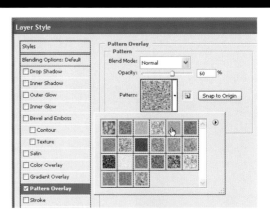

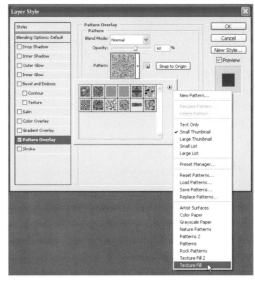

2 Set the blend mode to Vivid Light and reduce the opacity to 60%. Burlap is just one of the preset patterns that come with Photoshop—there are many, many others to choose from. You can also create your own pattern tile, either with original artwork or with a texture lifted from another image.

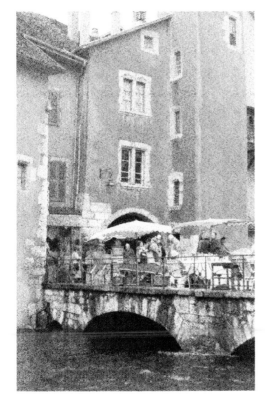

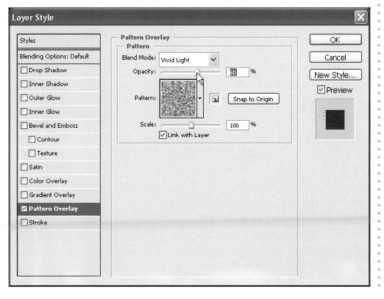

121

Infrared film effects

The use of infrared film was originally developed in the scientific community, but it is also used for artistic purposes. The characteristics of infrared photography lend a surreal, haunting quality to an image, which is why it has become so popular with art photographers.

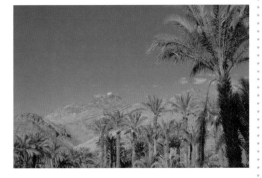

A dramatic, artistic look

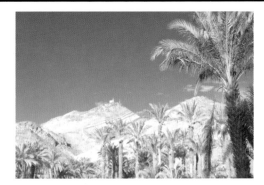

1 We are going to begin by making a mock grayscale image by using adjustment layers. (Until we have gone through all of the required steps, it will be difficult to assess what the contrast settings will need to be, so using adjustment layers will allow us to fine-tune the image at the very end.) Apply a Channel Mixer adjustment layer to the background layer. When the Channel Mixer dialog box opens, increase the percentage of the Red and Green channels, then decrease the percentage of the Blue channel. This creates a winter-like effect with snow-covered mountains (if you disregard the palm trees!).

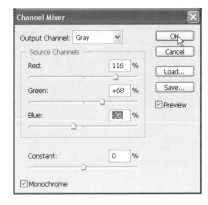

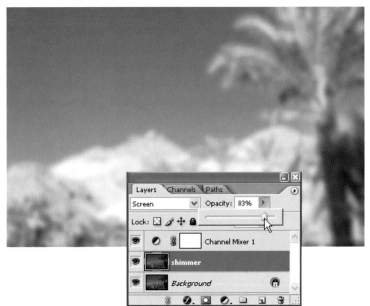

2 Duplicate the background layer, making sure the duplicate remains below the adjustment layer. Name the new layer "shimmer." To recreate the shimmering effect of infrared film, apply a Gaussian Blur (**Filter > Blur> Gaussian Blur**). Set the Radius to 8.0. Change the shimmer layer's blend mode to Screen, and reduce opacity to 83%.

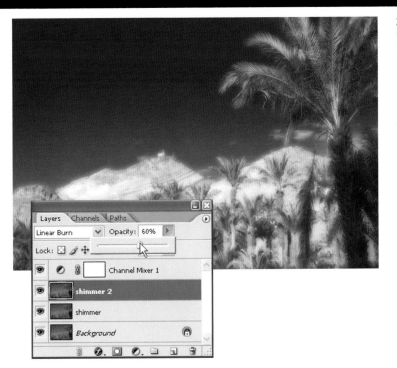

3 Now, duplicate the shimmer layer, ensuring that the copy remains below the Channel Mixer adjustment layer. Rename the layer "shimmer 2", change the layer mode to Linear Burn, and set the opacity to 60%. The finished result has the quality of infrared film about it. Now we can get really creative and customize the look.

CHANNEL MIXER

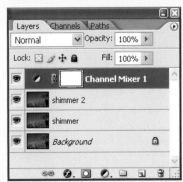

Using a Channel Mixer adjustment layer for creating grayscale images from color originals can provide many advantages over a straightforward grayscale conversion or desaturation. Select the Monochrome checkbox before you begin (see left), and experiment with the percentage settings for each of the Red, Blue, and Green channels to see the wide range of different effects and moods that can be obtained using this method.

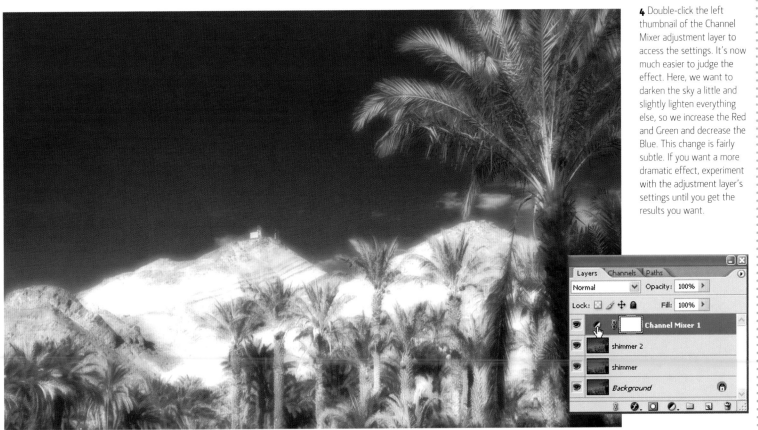

4 Double-click the left thumbnail of the Channel Mixer adjustment layer to access the settings. It's now much easier to judge the effect. Here, we want to darken the sky a little and slightly lighten everything else, so we increase the Red and Green and decrease the Blue. This change is fairly subtle. If you want a more dramatic effect, experiment with the adjustment layer's settings until you get the results you want.

Cross-processing

Cross-processing is another classic technique, in which slide film is processed using the chemistry normally reserved for a negative film, or (less often) where negative film is processed using slide film chemistry. The results are often unpredictable, but usually very interesting. With cross-processed slide film, you tend to get enhanced contrast, blown highlights and odd but interesting color shifts. Of course, Photoshop provides us with several more predictable routes to get a similar effect.

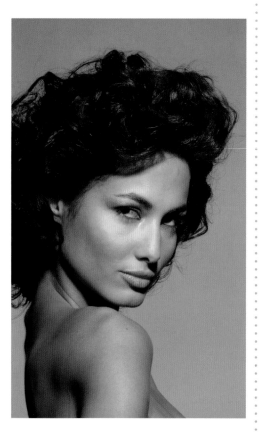

Method 1: **Curves**

Our first approach uses Curves. It's best to apply the Curves in an adjustment layer, as this enables you to go back later and tailor the results as you please. We'll try the technique on this simply lit portrait.

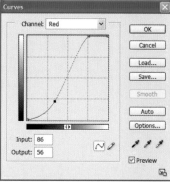

1 With the image open, either open a new Curves adjustment layer from the button at the bottom of the Layers palette, or select **Layer > New Adjustment Layer > Curves**. Select the Red channel from the drop-down in the Curves dialog. The Curve shown deepens the reds in the shadows and midtones.

2 Select the Green channel. This curve boosts the Greens across the board, allowing a strong color shift in the highlights, too.

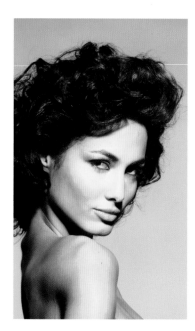

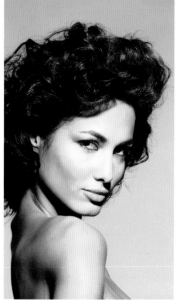

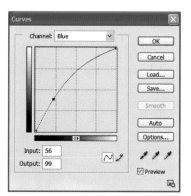

3 Now go to the Blue channel. This next Curve cools down the image, increasing the levels of blue in the skin tone, eyes, and hair highlights.

This second method uses a Gradient Map to create the unusual color shifts we associate with cross-processing. In some respects, this technique is more authentic, in that it's harder to predict and control the effects. These will vary depending on the image, and the Gradient Map or blending mode selected.

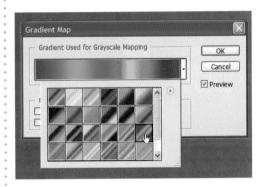

1 First, create a new Gradient Map adjustment layer. Feel free to try different Gradient Maps, but think about the colors in the image and try and find something that either contrasts or complements the existing palette. In this case, we're using a Gradient Map from the Color Harmonies 2 set. Click the arrow next to the pull-down selection if you need to load this set. Applied as is, the result looks awful.

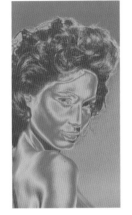

2 The trick is to change the blend mode and opacity of the adjustment layer. Color, Hue, and Overlay all provide good results with the opacity dropped to 50% or below. Here's the result with the blend mode set to Color and the opacity at 45%.

3 Hard Light, Linear Light, Color Burn, Color Dodge, and Pin Light produce a stronger effect, so the opacity may need to be lowered further. Here it is set to Color Dodge at 30% opacity, and Linear Light at 15% opacity.

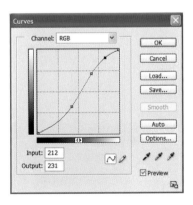

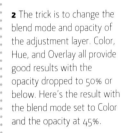

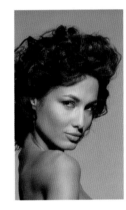

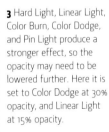

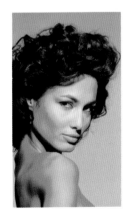

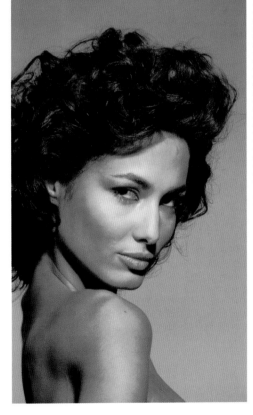

4 The colors are all there, but the contrast needs a boost. Select the RGB channel and apply a slight S-shaped contrast curve. This produces the final, oversaturated, slightly blown-out effect.

125

Hand-tinting

The process of hand-tinting black-and-white photographs became fashionable prior to the advent of widespread color printing. Rather than being a true-to-life reproduction of the original color scene, hand-tinting developed into a style of its own, and today epitomizes an entire era in the ongoing history of photography. While the effect will work with any kind of image, it lends itself best to portraits and scenes with a pre-1950s feel.

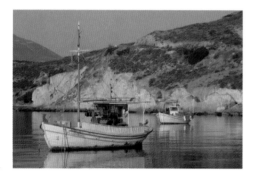

Recreating a classic style

1 To hand-tint a color image, we first need to remove the existing color. We want the color mode to be RGB, since we will be painting in color, so converting the mode to Grayscale won't work. Instead, press Ctrl/Cmd + U to desaturate without changing the color mode.

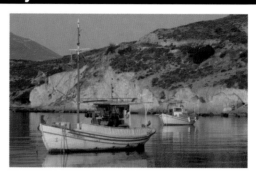

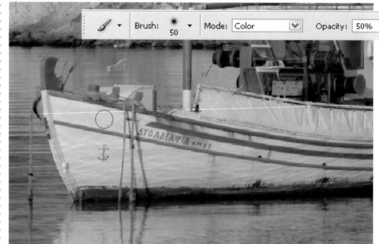

2 Now choose the Brush tool and set the mode to Color and the opacity to 50% using the Tool Options bar at the top of the screen. Choose a color and start to paint over the hull of the boat. Because we are in Color mode, the textures still show through the color of the paint.

3 We could continue doing it this way, but there is an alternative method that works better if you are painting larger areas. It follows the same principle but utilizes layer blend modes instead. To begin, create a new layer above the background layer. Name it "painting layer" and set its blend mode to Color. Select the Paintbrush tool and set the painting mode to Normal, using the Tool Options bar. Choose a color and start to paint onto the new paint layer. You can paint over textures and different shades without losing the detail, only changing the color.

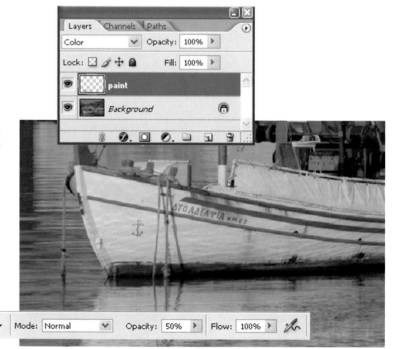

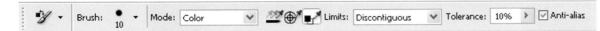

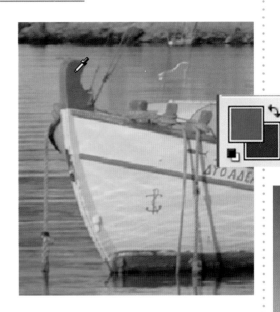

4 Let's try another method. The Color Replacement tool is commonly used to replace an existing color with another of your choosing. Used for hand-tinting, this tool offers us some options that can make the task a bit less tedious. First, select the Eyedropper tool (to use the keyboard shortcut, just press I). Sample the dark area of the wood above the bows as shown. Press x on the keyboard so the color you just sampled becomes the background color.

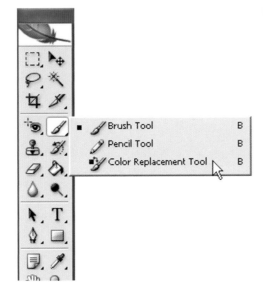

Brush Tool   B
Pencil Tool   B
Color Replacement Tool   B

5 Now choose the Color Replacement tool, go up to the Tool Options bar, and apply the settings shown. Setting the Sampling drop-down to Background Swatch, we can paint over the required area without paint spilling over the edge. The Mode is set to Color, which works the same way as in the previous methods. Limits is set to Discontiguous, which will replace the sampled color anytime the cursor encounters it. Tolerance defines the range of colors to be replaced, from 0 to 255. Higher values increase the range of colors.

6 Choose a color and paint over the wooden area. You will find that even if you run over the edge of the area designated, the paint will not overrun the edges. As long as the pixels remain within the tolerance of the background swatch, the color will be contained. Continue using a combination of these techniques, but don't feel you have to tint every element of the photo. Often the result is more effective if some parts of the image remain untinted.

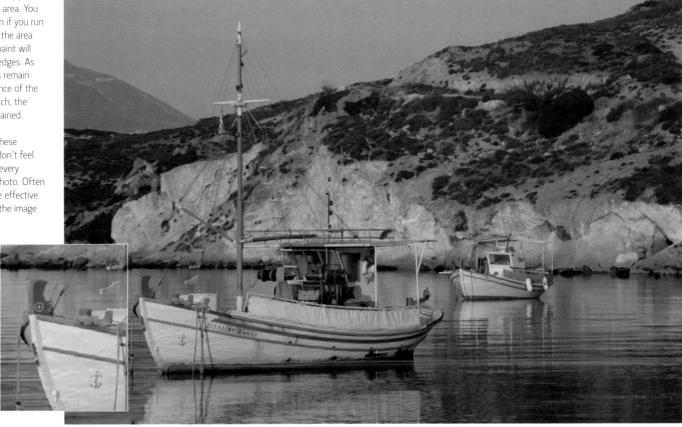

Posterization effects

To posterize an image is to print or display it using only a limited number of tones. The effect has its negative, undesirable side. For instance, when an image is badly manipulated, posterization can creep in, creating horrible banding artifacts and limiting the dynamic tonal range. But posterization also has creative applications—and it's invaluable when replicating a silk-screened effect.

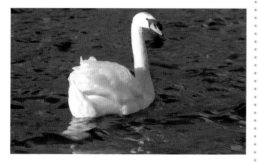

Method 1: **The Posterize command**

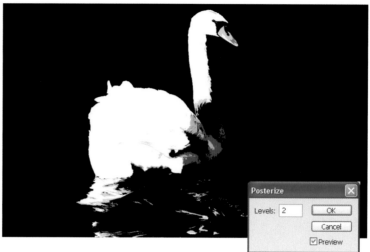

1 The Posterize dialog box gives you the option to select a number of Levels. It's important not to confuse this with the number of final colors, as it actually refers to tonal or brightness values. If we set the Levels to 2, it translates as two per channel, so in an RGB image, we get two colors for each of the Red, Green, and Blue channels, giving us a total of six. The result may or may not be what you are looking for, and this is the command's weakness: there's not enough control over the amount or choice of colors.

Photoshop includes a dedicated posterization function which delivers some interesting color effects—but perhaps with not quite enough control over the final result.

Method 2: **Grayscale posterization**

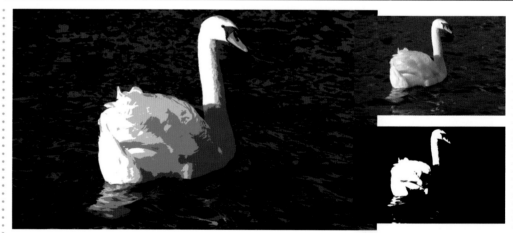

For greater control and a better result, start with a grayscale image. It doesn't need to be true grayscale: just desaturate the original color image by pressing Ctrl/Cmd + Shift + U. Any other method will also work fine.

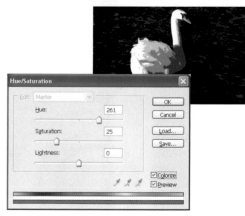

1 Apply the Posterize command with 2 levels again and we get what looks like a 1-bit image or just black-and-white. We need more detail, so return to the original grayscale image and reapply the Posterize command, this time with 5 levels.

2 All that is required now is some color. Press Ctrl/Cmd + U for Hue/Saturation. Check the Colorize box and drag the Hue slider to get your chosen color. The result is a more suitable basis for a screen print, with total control over the color chosen.

128

Method 3: **Gradient Map**

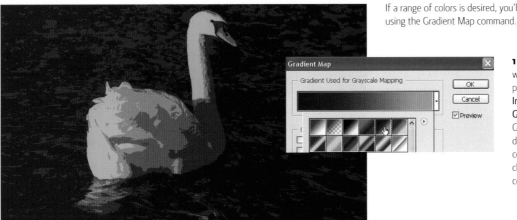

If a range of colors is desired, you'll achieve better results by using the Gradient Map command.

1 Starting with the image we created in step 1 of the previous method, go to **Image > Adjustments > Gradient Map**. Choose a Gradient from the drop-down or mix your own colors. The potential is clear—it's up to you how complex the image becomes.

Method 4: **The Cutout filter**

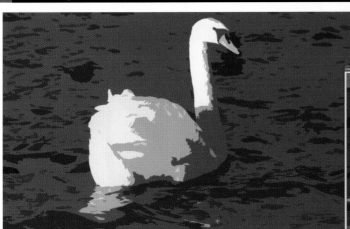

An alternative method is to use one of the artistic filters. Return to the original color image, and this time go to **Filter > Artistic > Cutout**.

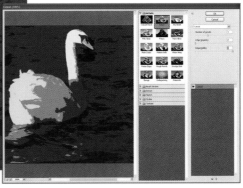

1 The number of Levels you choose defines the number of colors in the image. Keep the Edge Simplicity at 0 and Edge Fidelity at 3. The result is similar to the Posterize command, but this time we are using the original colors in the image.

129

Method 5: **Indexed color**

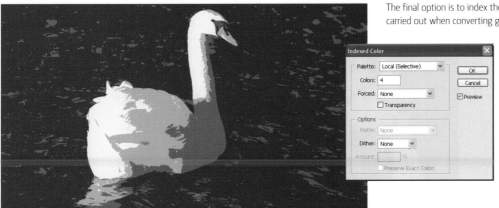

The final option is to index the image (a process usually carried out when converting graphics for the Web).

1 Using the original color image, go to **Image > Mode > Indexed Color**. Layered files will need to be flattened, so use a duplicate if you want to keep any layers intact. Choose a setting of 4 colors with the Dither drop-down set to None. This ensures flat blocks of color. If you want to use a gradient map to color the image, you will have to change the mode back to RGB. This won't change how the image looks, but it will allow you to use all the filters, commands, and layers again.

Classic print effects

Rock and pop stars, film idols, sports heroes, and even revolutionary figureheads have had the treatment. Andy Warhol is synonymous with it—if you type Che Guevara into any search engine, the first thing that will come up is the famous '60s poster. The flat, cutout effect is beloved of poster printers and music and film packagers, and Photoshop makes it easy to create.

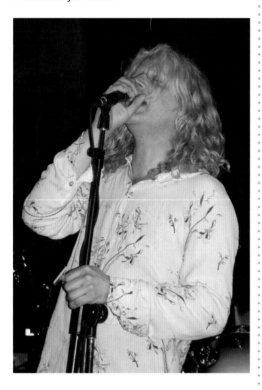

This photograph of a rock singer makes a good starting point for a successful poster image.

1 Go to **Image** > **Adjustments** > **Threshold**. Threshold creates an image comprised of black and white pixels only. The slider allows you to set a value from 1 to 255, where any pixels lighter than the Threshold value are converted to white, and pixels darker than the Threshold value are converted to black. In its raw state, it may not give the effect that you visualize. Here, for instance, we want a very detailed black-and-white image. At a Threshold value of 85, the hair has the right amount of detail, but most of the other detail is washed out.

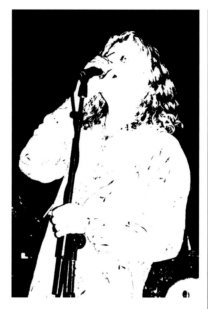

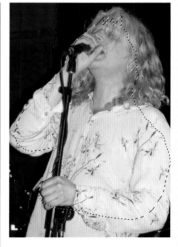

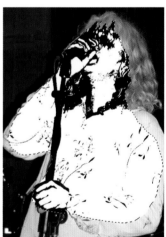

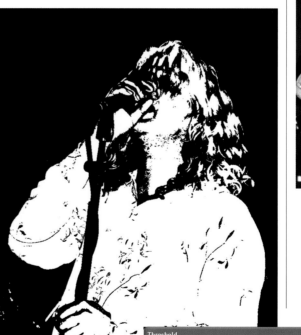

2 We can fix this. Before applying Threshold, make a selection of the areas where we want to preserve detail. Now apply Threshold with a value of 126.

3 Invert the selection (Ctrl/Cmd + Shift + I) and apply Threshold again with a value of 86. A whole image can be built up in this way, using selections to preserve detail where it's needed.

Method 2: **Calculations**

Another method for producing the same kind of effect is to use a command that combines channels.

1 Go to **Image** > **Calculations**. Change the blend mode to Hard Mix and the Red channel for Sources 1 and 2. Set the Result drop-down to New Document. The result is similar to the result we got using Method 1.

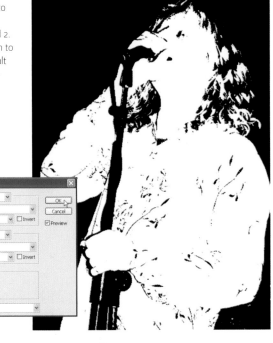

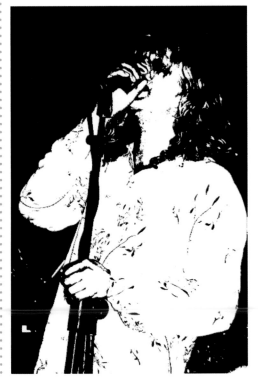

2 By blending different channels from Sources 1 and 2, different black-and-white effects will result. Here, the Red and Blue channels have been blended.

Although it's easy enough to color the results of these black-and-white methods, it's generally better to create color versions using Photoshop's Cutout filter. Go to **Filter** > **Artistic** > **Cutout**. The settings shown are designed to capture the maximum detail from the image. The result is posterization, which we covered in more detail on pages 128-129.

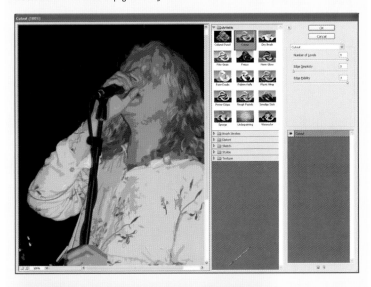

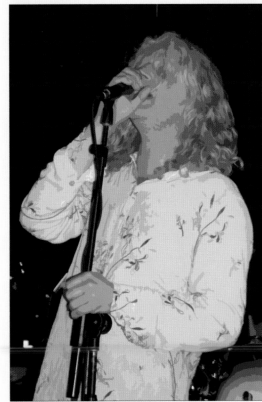

Solarization effects

In its purest form, solarization is a process whereby a photographic image is overexposed under an intense light source. After some time, a reversal occurs, resulting in an image that is part negative, part positive. This process, sometimes described as reversal solarization, is performed using a single exposure.

The similar Sabatier effect works slightly differently. In the mid-19th century, it was observed that a second exposure of a partially developed plate would cause a reversal to parts of or the whole negative. It was a doctor by the name of Sabatier who wrote of this effect in 1860—though he was not the first to document it—and it is the Sabatier effect that most people refer to when they describe solarization in creative photographic terms.

Solarization in photography came of age with its use by the surrealist Man Ray. While the process works in color, it's still identified with his brand of haunting, enigmatic, black-and-white imagery.

Photoshop has a dedicated solarization filter which works by blending positive and negative versions of the image. However, there are other methods of creating this effect.

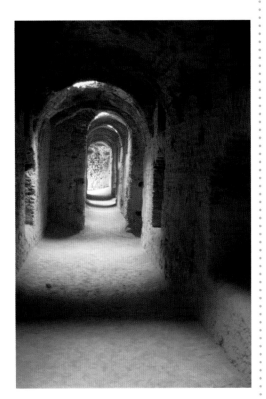

Method 1: **Solarization**

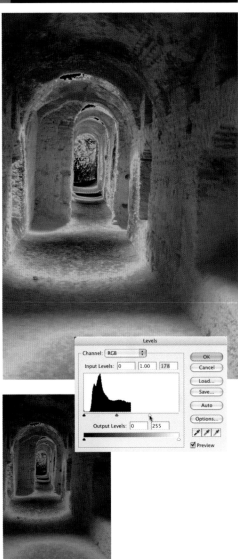

For this method, start with a black-and-white image with a nice range of tones. If you don't have a suitable black-and-white image, you can always Desaturate a color image by pressing Ctrl/Cmd + Shift + U.

1 To use the Solarization filter, go to **Filter > Stylize > Solarize**. You will notice that the Shadows and Midtones remain positive while the highlights become negative.

2 The image can be further enhanced by using any of the brightness or contrast tools. Try Levels, dragging the white point left to lighten the image.

Method 2: **Invert and Darken**

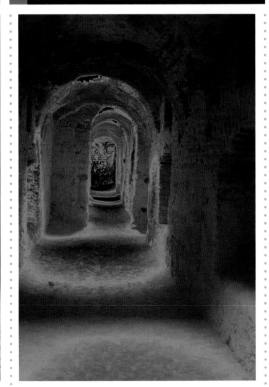

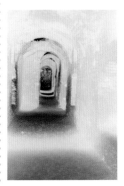

1 Let's try another way to achieve the same effect. Duplicate the layer, then go to Image > Adjustments > Invert or press Ctrl/Cmd + I to make a negative version.

2 This doesn't truly emulate the solarization effect, as the entire image is now a negative. To bring the shadows and midtones back to positive, change the blend mode to Darken.

Method 3: **Gradient Map**

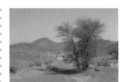

1 This method works straight on color images without the need for a black-and-white conversion. It also allows for more fine-tuning on the final look of the image. Go to **Image > Adjustments > Gradient Map**, and use a three-color gradient from white to dark gray to white. The result has a strong atmospheric feel.

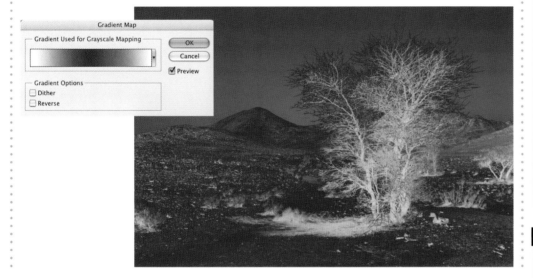

Method 4: **Exclusion with Luminosity mask**

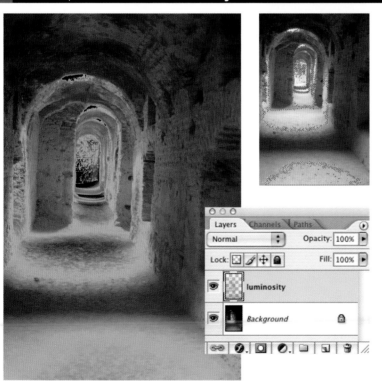

1 Preserving the shadows and midtones while darkening the highlights is a constant concern in all of these techniques. In this method, we'll isolate the brightest areas automatically by using a luminosity mask. Windows users can press Ctrl + Alt + Shift + ~ (Mac users, press Cmd + Opt + ~). We now have a selection of the image luminosity. Press Ctrl/Cmd + J to copy and paste the selection to a new layer, and change the luminosity layer's blend mode to Exclusion.

2 Use Levels to lighten the background layer if necessary.

ALTERNATIVES

To view an alternative version, make a duplicate of the background layer. Apply the same gradient map, but this time enable the Reverse checkbox. The result is a very different image.

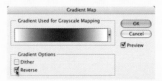

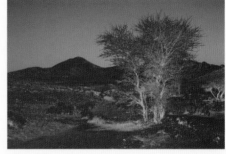

CUSTOMIZATION

For the ultimate in customization, when you first choose the gradient, double-click in the Preview window of the Gradient Map dialog box to bring up the Gradient Editor. Now you can change every aspect of the gradient—color, type, smoothness, and color range. You can also see the effect this has on the image, live, as you make adjustments.

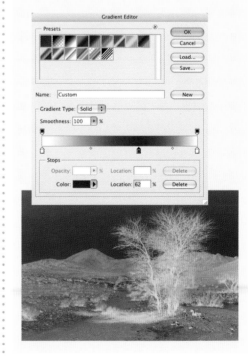

133

Mezzotints

Mezzotints were highly popular in the 17th, 18th, and early 19th centuries as a method for reproducing black-and-white paintings and illustrations. The technique involved the use of a steel or copper plate which had been engraved so that the rough areas represented shadow and the smooth areas represented light. The style was open to a high diversity of interpretations, and for this reason Photoshop's own Mezzotint filter may not fit everyone's idea of what a mezzotint should be. As a result, we'll look at Photoshop's rendition of the style, but also at other methods with a little more opportunity for creative license. The choice of image is paramount, particularly if you are using the mezzotint filter. Bold, simple images work best, and high contrast originals will help ensure that the final result is recognizable.

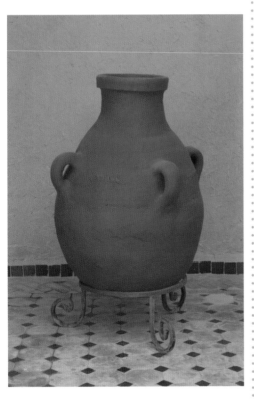

Method 1: **The Mezzotint filter**

Let's begin with Photoshop's own Mezzotint filter.

1 Go to **Filter** > **Pixelate** > **Mezzotint**. Choose a style from the Type drop-down and click OK. You can be the judge of the result.

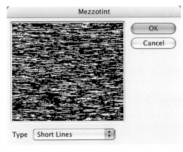

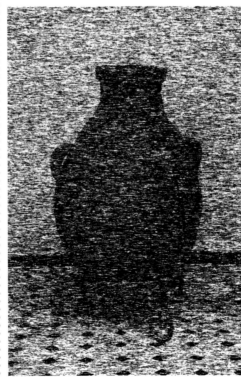

Method 2: **Film Grain and Graphic Pen**

If that's not quite what you are looking for, there are other options. Copy the original urn file, open the copy and duplicate the background layer. Rename the layers "film noise" (bottom) and "graphic pen" (top).

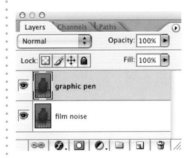

1 Hide the graphic pen layer and activate the film noise layer. Now go to **Filter** > **Artistic** > **Film Grain** and apply the settings shown.

2 Now activate the graphic pen layer and go to **Filter** > **Sketch** > **Graphic Pen**. I've chosen the longest stroke length with a mid-range light/dark balance, but you can be creative here if you are looking for something different.

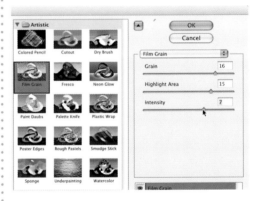

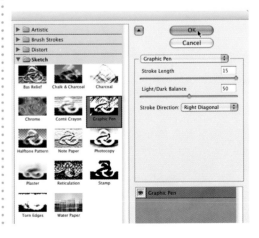

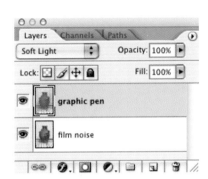

3 Finally, change the graphic pen layer's blend mode to Soft Light.

4 We could leave it at this stage, but I want to bring out the diagonal strokes and tone down the colors to create an effect closer to that of an engraving. Make sure the graphic pen layer is still active and go to **Image> Adjustments> Gradient Map**. If necessary, load the Metals gradient set, and choose the Silver option.

5 This is closer to the true tradition of the art, preserving the detail of the image and the light and shadow while minimizing the telltale signs of computer intervention. By experimenting with the settings yourself, you will be able to achieve a wide array of styles, each with your own personal feel.

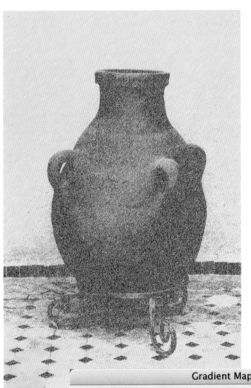

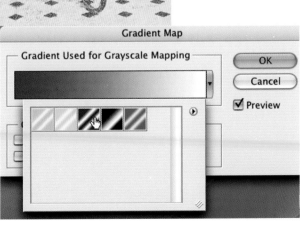

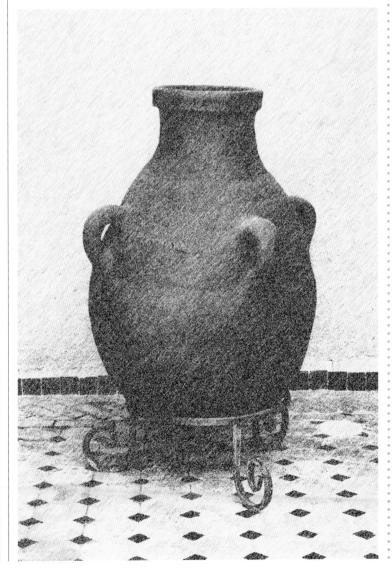

Reticulation effects

Reticulation refers to the effect created when photographic film emulsion encounters a radical change of temperature at critical points during the development process. The cracking and warping of the emulsion causes the image to manifest with fine grain in the highlights and a heavier, globular look in the shadows.

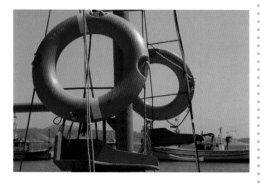

Method 1: **The Reticulation filter**

Photoshop has its own Reticulation filter, which works best on images that feature strong, bold shapes. This is a perfect example.

1 Set the foreground and background colors to define new colors for the image. Blues, grays and browns are good for an antique effect, but feel free to experiment with other colors. Now, go to **Filter > Sketch > Reticulation**. Foreground and Background level sliders indicate which, if any, of the colors has prominence. Higher values result in a greater spread of the color. Adjust the Density slider for the amount of texture.

2 Although you have a certain amount of control over the result, you may want to customize the effect more to your own taste. Next, we'll work through a manual technique for reticulation.

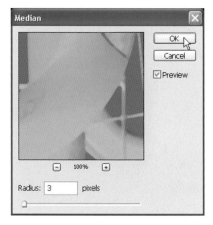

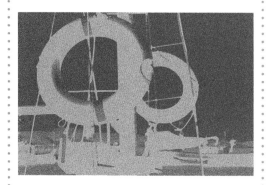

Method 2: **Patterns and Gradient Maps**

Although the Reticulation filter gives you some control over the final result, this manual technique offers more room for customization.

1 First, we'll use a Gradient Map to define the colors. Choose two colors that contrast well for the foreground and background colors, with the lighter color as the foreground. Go to **Image > Adjustments > Gradient Map**.

2 Although this isn't a very detailed image, it will work better with even less detail. To flatten it further, go to **Filter > Noise > Median** and apply a value of 3.

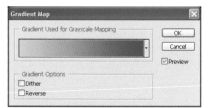

3 For a realistic effect, we want the highlights to contain a fine grain while the rest of the image develops the clumped look associated with reticulation. To isolate the highlights, go to **Select > Color Range**. Choose Highlights from the Select drop-down.

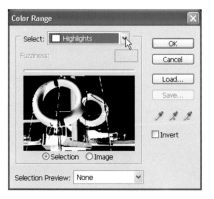

4 To avoid any sharp distinctions, the selection needs further feathering. Press Ctrl/Cmd + Alt + D for the Feather command and enter a value of 20 pixels. Now press Ctrl/Cmd + J to copy and paste the selection to a new layer.

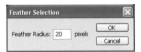

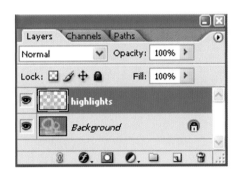

5 Double-click the background layer and rename it "shadows/midtones." We need do this because we are going to apply a Layer Style pattern, which won't work on a background layer.

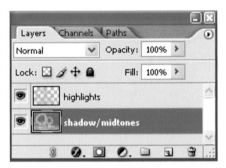

6 With the shadows/midtones layer active, click the Layer Style icon at the bottom of the Layers palette, and choose Pattern Overlay. If not already loaded, load the pattern set called "Texture Fill" by clicking the pop-up button at the top right of the pattern swatches. Choose the pattern called "Burlap" from the swatches. Set the blend mode to Overlay and scale to 180%, then click OK.

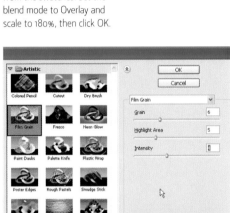

7 Activate the Highlights layer and go to **Filter > Artistic > Film Grain** to apply the fine grain where it's needed.

137

8 The grain filter has left the highlights with a dark wash over them. Press Ctrl/Cmd + L for levels and drag the white slider to the left to lighten the highlights. The settings we have been using are a matter of taste. Experiment with different grain settings and even different patterns for the shadows and midtones for a variety of creative effects.

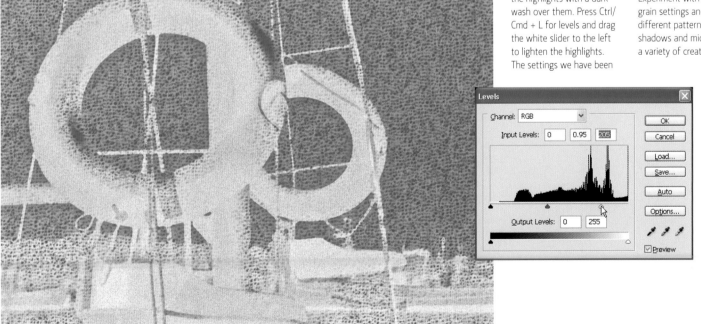

PROCESSING RAW FILES

Working with RAW images

Working with RAW images

In essence, a RAW file is a digital negative: a file containing all the raw sensor data from the camera, along with information on the settings used. Photoshop's Camera RAW plug-in becomes the digital darkroom and gives you the controls to convert this data into a finished image, just as a photo lab would with a film negative in a traditional darkroom.

Using RAW files provides many benefits, including complete control over the most commonly applied adjustments, such as sharpness, color, brightness, contrast, color balance and white balance settings. On the downside, the image is much larger than the more common JPG format (though smaller than a TIFF format) and can't be opened without a converter (either an application supplied by the manufacturer or the Camera RAW plug-in) to interpret the data as an image. Still, the advantages of having a RAW file with its almost infinite control over the final output makes it the format of choice in a professional environment, or in any situation where quality and flexibility issues outweigh speed.

Opening RAW images

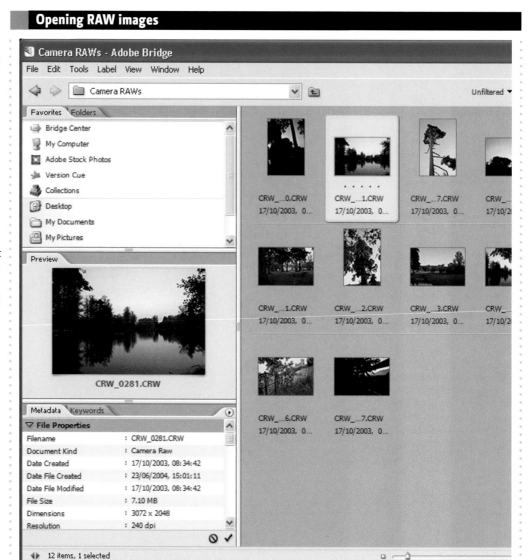

1 First, download your images to a folder on your hard disk, then use Photoshop's File Browser (or Adobe Bridge as it's called in CS2) to navigate to the relevant folder. It's also possible to process a RAW image by using the **File > Open** command, but the File Browser is far more flexible when reviewing a batch of files. If you have a number of files in the folder, it may take a while for all the image previews to appear.

2 To open an image for processing, double-click its thumbnail. This action opens a large preview of the image in a dialog box, and it's here that all the processing decisions are made.

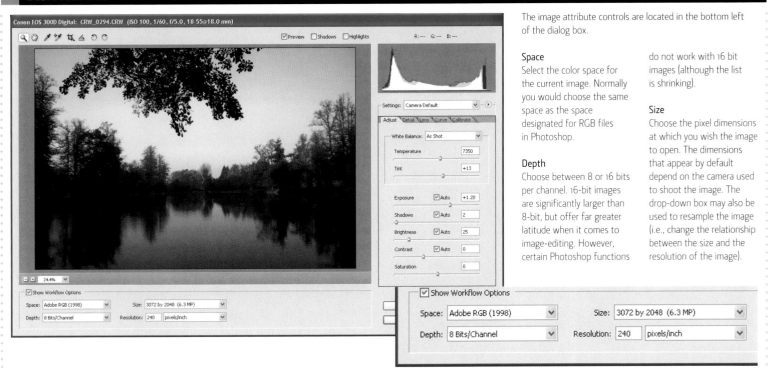

The image attribute controls are located in the bottom left of the dialog box.

Space

Select the color space for the current image. Normally you would choose the same space as the space designated for RGB files in Photoshop.

Depth

Choose between 8 or 16 bits per channel. 16-bit images are significantly larger than 8-bit, but offer far greater latitude when it comes to image-editing. However, certain Photoshop functions do not work with 16 bit images (although the list is shrinking).

Size

Choose the pixel dimensions at which you wish the image to open. The dimensions that appear by default depend on the camera used to shoot the image. The drop-down box may also be used to resample the image (i.e., change the relationship between the size and the resolution of the image).

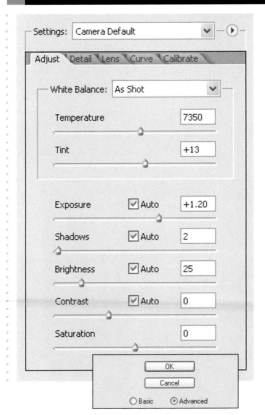

The options don't stop there. Click the Advanced tab to reveal the full range of parameters that can be adjusted. Four tabs provide access to the basic and advanced settings. The first one is the Adjust tab.

Adjust

White Balance

Refers to the type of lighting under which the image was taken and therefore defines the color balance of the image. If your camera's white balance setting can be read by the RAW plug-in, you can choose As Shot to use the camera's own white balance setting. Otherwise using this setting will render the same result as an Auto setting. You're not obliged to use the white balance setting that was in operation at the time the image was taken—for creative reasons, you might prefer a different quality of light. Using a different white balance now would be the same as choosing that setting at the time the photograph was taken.

Temperature

As the white balance is changed, the temperature changes accordingly. In this context, "temperature" refers to color temperature (measured in degrees Kelvin). Lower temperatures render a progressively bluer image, while higher values gravitate towards yellow.

Tint

The tint can be used in conjunction with the temperature setting as a method of finely adjusting the Kelvin setting.

Exposure

Controls the brightness of the image. The numeric field relates to f-stops on the camera. A setting of +1.00 is equivalent to opening the shutter by one stop on the camera. Using the exposure slider is an excellent way to recapture lost detail in highlights.

Shadows

Similar to adjusting the black slider in levels. Higher values will darken the shadows as more pixels become mapped to black.

Brightness

Similar to exposure but with one major difference: this setting does not clip the highlights or shadows, which means pixels will not be mapped to white in the highlights or black in the shadows. This setting is generally used as a fine adjustment after the exposure and shadow settings have been confirmed.

Contrast

Increases or decreases contrast by making a midtone adjustment, therefore not affecting the absolute highlights or shadows.

Saturation

Enriches colors by dragging the slider to the right, or drag left to desaturate.

Working with RAW images

Advanced features continued

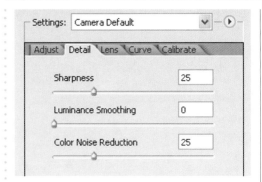

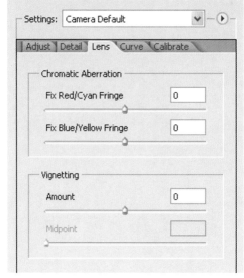

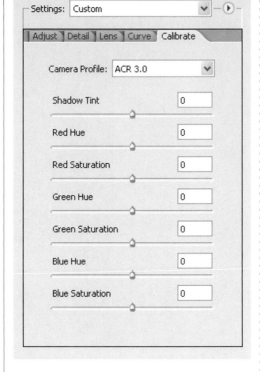

Detail
Sharpness
You will need to zoom to 100% or more to able to gauge the result accurately. Sharpness works in the same way as the Unsharp Mask filter. Drag the slider to the right to increase sharpening, or drag left to decrease it. Use lower settings for less dramatic results. If you are planning to edit the image further in Photoshop, the feature can be turned off by applying a setting of zero. You can always use the Unsharp Mask filter later.

Sharpening can be applied to the image or to the preview only. To determine how sharpening is applied, click the pop-up menu button to the right of the settings drop-down box and choose Preferences. Then select the required option from the second drop-down box.

The next two settings are used as a method of noise reduction. High ISO settings and less-capable cameras are both factors in the generation of unwanted noise. Before changing the settings, zoom into the image so you can see the results more clearly.

Luminance Smoothing
Refers to grayscale noise, which manifests as a grainy effect in the image. Shift the slider to the right to reduce this.

Color Noise Reduction
Refers to chroma or color noise. This often appears as colored artifacts, such as patterns or clear pixels of color. In any case, drag the slider to the right to reduce noise. A value of zero disables the function.

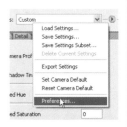

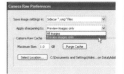

Lens
Chromatic Aberration
Chromatic Aberration is a misregistration of colors in the CCD, resulting in red and cyan fringing or even blue/yellow fringing in extreme cases. To see the effect, zoom in very closely to a very light/dark, high contrast area in a corner of the image. If the image suffers from chromatic aberration, it will be visible here. To remove red/cyan fringing, drag the Chromatic Aberration R/C (red/cyan) slider right or left and preview the result as you drag until it is minimized or reduced. For blue/yellow fringing, do the same with the B/Y (blue/yellow) slider.

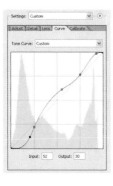

Vignetting
Describes a lens anomaly where the edges and corner of the image are darker than the center. Move the Vignetting Amount slider to the right to lighten corners and to the left to darken them. Making an adjustment to this slider automatically enables the Midpoint slider.

Vignetting midpoint slider
Dragging this slider to the right constrains the adjustment to the corners. Drag left to enable a wider area of influence away from the corners.

Curve
The Curve tab (new to Photoshop CS2) works effectively like the Curves dialog with the RGB Composite channel selected in Photoshop, enabling a vast range of tonal adjustments before you even get into Photoshop proper. Up to 16 points can be set for adjustment, and Linear, Medium Contrast, and Strong Contrast presets can be selected from the Tone Curve drop-down.

Calibrate
Shadow Tint
This slider can be used after all of the previous adjustments to remove any color casts that persist in the shadow areas. The colors affected relate back to the camera's sensor and the white balance setting. Dragging the slider to the left adds green to the shadows. Dragging right adds magenta.

Red, Green, Blue Hue
If colors in your image don't meet your expectations, it may be due to differences between the camera profile and the plug-in's profile for

that camera. In this situation, the three Hue sliders allow you to make to non-neutral colors. Drag the slider to the right to push the hue clockwise through the color wheel; drag left to cycle counter-clockwise.

Red, Green, Blue Saturation
After setting the hues, drag the Saturation slider to the right to saturate colors, and left to desaturate them.

Finished?
Click OK to process and open the image. Save the opened image in the desired format.

142

PHOTOSHOP RAW, CAMERA RAW & DNG

Although there is a .raw file format in Photoshop, is it not the same as the original Camera RAW image format. While this may be a bit confusing, it's worth being aware of. It may help to think of the camera RAW file as a digital negative, worth archiving in its original format.

In an effort to create a more standardized digital negative format, Adobe has introduced its own with Photoshop CS2. The DNG format converts the files from the many different Camera RAW formats used by camera manufacturers into a standard format for archiving and processing, and is the default option when you save from the RAW plug-in in Photoshop CS2.

Settings can be saved and used again for a certain camera or a specific lighting condition. Subsets can also be saved, in which case only certain adjustments will be applied. You decide how the setting will be saved, either as an entry in the Camera RAW database file, or as a Sidecar XMP file.

Camera RAW database
Storing the settings in the database has the benefit that the settings are indexed by file content rather than name, which means you can transfer files anywhere on the computer and even rename a file without losing the associated settings. Please note that this only works when you are transferring files from one place to another on the same computer. As soon as you move the files to another computer or storage device, the settings will no longer be associated.

Sidecar XMP files
This option stores the settings in an XMP (Extensible Metadata Platform) file in the same folder as the raw file, using the same name and an XMP extension. This is the preferred option for transferring RAW files and their associated settings onto CD or DVD or within a network of computers. It is also a better option within a multiple-user setup where files and settings need to be shared.

1 To designate how settings should be saved, click the pop-up menu button next to the Settings drop-down box and choose Preferences. Then choose the required option from the first drop-down box.

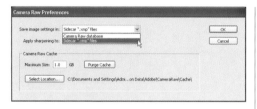

2 Once you've determined what the settings should be, save them by choosing Save Settings from the pop-up menu button. Choose a descriptive name for the file, and be sure to save it in the camera RAW folder.

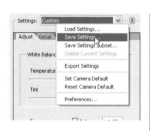

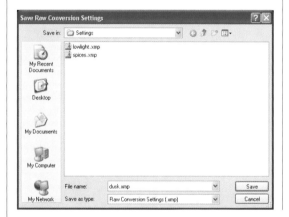

3 The saved setting now appears in the Settings drop-down box, along with the standard settings and any other custom settings you may create. Any of the saved settings in the drop-down box can be applied to an image. Each of these settings can also be used as a default set for any image from the same camera. Just click the Settings pop-up menu, select a setting, and then choose Set Camera Default.

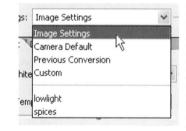

143

TIP

AUTOMATE OPENING RAW FILES
Opening a RAW image takes time—a lot more time than opening a JPEG. For this reason, you may wish to use Photoshop's automated commands as you would with any of Photoshop's more labor-intensive operations. Using an action to perform all of the steps required to open a RAW file puts the computer to work—and frees you up for something more productive. When recording an action, it is best to use Selected Image in the Settings drop-down box. This ensures that each image's own settings will be used to open the file.

PHOTO RESTORATION

Removing dust and scratches

Removing moiré patterns from scans

Revitalizing faded photographs

Recreating damaged areas

Antique effects

Removing dust and scratches

When we talk about dust and scratches, we're talking about any small, unwanted artifact that might appear in a digital or digitized photograph. These artifacts stem from a range of sources, from specks on the lens or in the camera to material picked up in the film development or scanning process. Whatever the source, our task is to remove them seamlessly, without much effort.

Of course, a bit of work with a duster and blower brush before you scan can save you a lot of time afterwards, but, failing that, there are several options for removing dust digitally. When faced with removing single scratches from an image, the tendency is to reach for the Clone Stamp, Healing Brush, Spot Healing Brush, and Patch tools. When dealing with a profusion of smaller debris, however, wholesale methods of removal are called for.

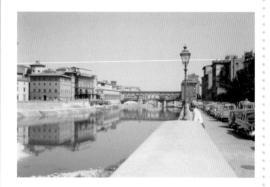

Using Filters

This scan from a 40-year-old transparency is peppered with a liberal scattering of artifacts, but they are most noticeable in the sky, water, and the foreground area.

1 The detail and texture of the area that needs cleaning up will dictate which method to use. Where the area is fairly uniform, as in the sky, we can use a simple blur. First, make a feathered selection of the area, then go to **Filter > Blur > Gaussian Blur**. Using a Radius setting of 9.5 pixels, you will see the marks virtually disappear with the exception of one larger persistent black mark on the left.

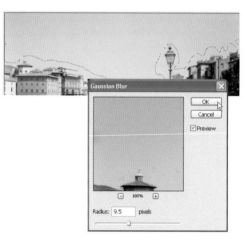

2 The black mark visible just above the buildings in the next image demonstrates one of the limitations of using Gaussian Blur to clean up images: in areas of significant contrast, it may not be particularly effective. Undo the Gaussian Blur and go to **Filter > Noise > Dust and Scratches**. A Radius setting of about 13 will clean up the sky, and will also take care of the black mark.

3 The stone area in the foreground also has some very discernible debris. Make a selection of this area, and re-open the Dust and Scratches filter. A 13-pixel Radius clears the debris, but also removes some of the texture and shading.

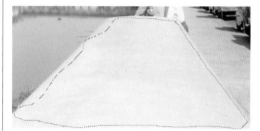

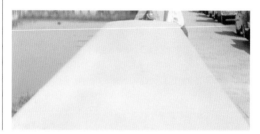

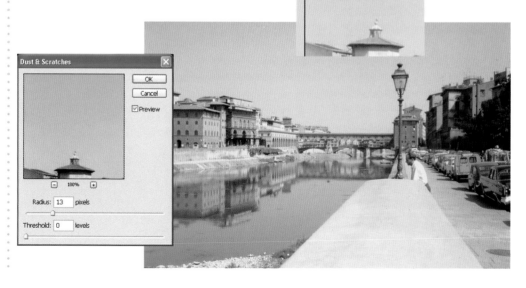

4 That's where the Threshold setting comes in: it determines how different one pixel's value has to be from the others in its immediate radius before the filter will affect it. As the Threshold value is increased, fewer pixels are affected, returning the image to a state closer to its original and enabling the detail to show through. Push the Threshold value up until the main detail of the selection appears, but stop before the unwanted debris returns. A setting of 7 works well in this instance.

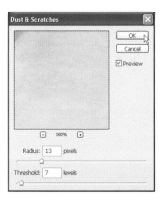

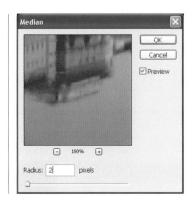

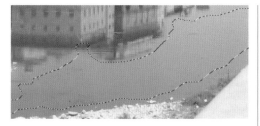

5 The last area to work on is the water. The debris isn't so obvious here, as there is a lot of shade and texture in the water to distract the eye. However, on closer inspection, you will see some very dark, prominent, black marks. Let's try another method. Start by making a selection of the water area to be worked on.

6 The Median filter is commonly used for reducing noise in an image by blending the brightness values of pixels. A blurring effect results, which can remove unwanted debris, given the right kind of image. Go to **Filter > Noise > Median** and apply a Radius of 2 pixels. This removes the obvious black marks, and while there is some slight blurring, it's not detrimental to the final image.

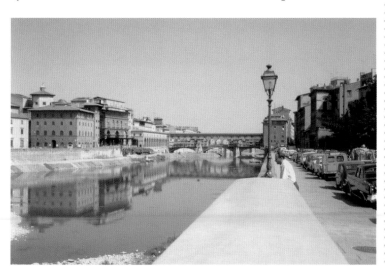

A MANUAL TECHNIQUE

If the filters prove inadequate, there's an old-fashioned manual method that suits more uniform areas, such as the heavily marked sky in this image.

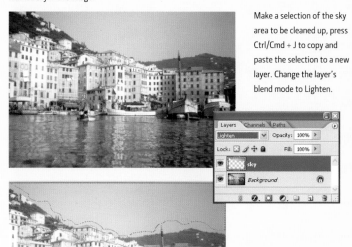

Make a selection of the sky area to be cleaned up, press Ctrl/Cmd + J to copy and paste the selection to a new layer. Change the layer's blend mode to Lighten.

Make sure the Move tool is active, then use the keyboard arrow keys to nudge the sky layer up by 6 pixels and left by 2 pixels. The actual amounts you nudge depend on the image and placement of the marks, but by setting the layer blend mode to Lighten before nudging, you can see the changes taking place.

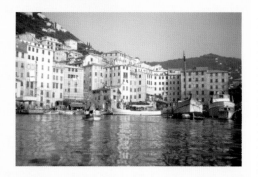

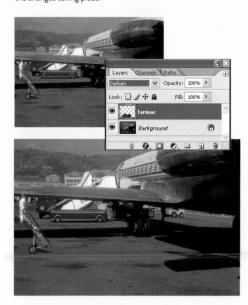

Lighten mode worked because we were removing dark pixels from a lighter background, but what if the marks we need to remove are light on a dark background? All you need to do is set the blend mode to Darken instead of Lighten.

147

Removing moiré patterns from scans

In the context of scanning, moiré describes a pattern that forms across an image when it has been scanned from a book or magazine. Most modern scanners have built-in functionality to deal with the problems of moiré, but Photoshop can also minimize the effect.

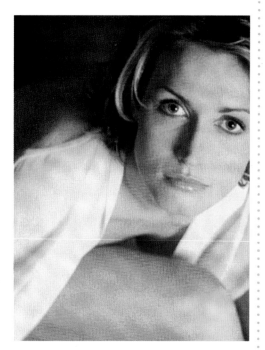

This image was scanned from a magazine and shows a moiré pattern which is particularly prevalent in the darker areas. Set the view to Actual Pixels (View > Actual Pixels), as you need to see exactly what you're dealing with.

1 The moiré pattern is more obvious on some channels than others. Looking through the channels, you'll find that the Blue channel is most heavily affected, with the Green and Red channels somewhat less so. By blurring the relevant channels in proportion to the intensity of the visible moiré pattern, we can minimize the amount of blur to the image as a whole, thus reducing the need for subsequent sharpening. With the Blue channel active, go to **Filter > Blur > Gaussian Blur**. You will need to judge how much blur to apply. In this instance a radius of 3.0 is sufficient to disguise the most obvious pattern without destroying too much clarity in the image.

2 Once again, you will need to judge whether you need to apply blurring to the remaining channels. In this image, the moiré is still quite significant in the Green and Red channels, so apply a radius of 1.5 to the Green channel and 1.9 to the Red Channel. Here's how the image looks after all three channels have been independently blurred.

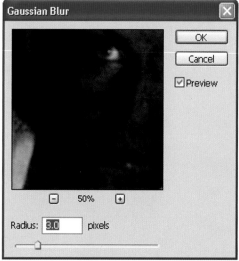

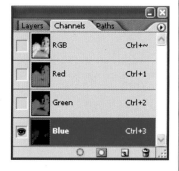

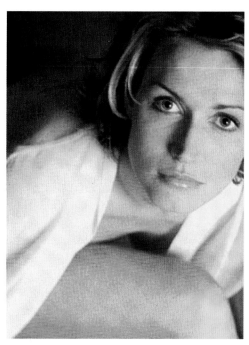

Tip

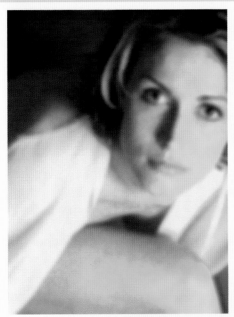

If you are wondering how this differs from applying the blur just once to the composite image, here is a comparison. The cumulative amount of blur we applied in the previous example equals 6.4. (3.0 + 1.9 +1.5). This example shows the original image with a Gaussian blur total radius of 6.4 applied once just to the composite image. The difference is startling, and clearly inferior to selective blurring of channels.

An alternative method is to convert the image to LAB mode: **Image > Mode > Lab Color**. Take a look at the Channels palette. In addition to the composite channel called Lab, you will see a Lightness channel and "a" and "b" channels.

1 The Lightness channel contains the detail of the image and the a and b channels hold the color components. Apply blurring to a, b, or both a and b channels depending on the need. The next example shows the image after Gaussian blurring of 3.0 has been applied to both the a and b channels. No additional sharpening was used. Although this process has reduced the moiré pattern, the previous method was actually more successful. However, that won't be the same for every image. Next time you encounter moiré, you can experiment with both.

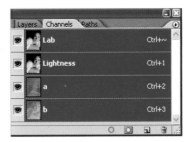

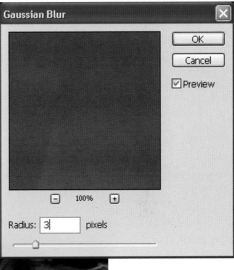

3 Now add a little sharpening to compensate for the blur. Go to **Filter > Sharpen > Unsharp Mask**. It's important to be conservative here or you risk intensifying any pattern remnants. You can judge by eye or use the settings shown. For a full explanation of the Unsharp Mask filter, see the section on sharpening images on page 37.

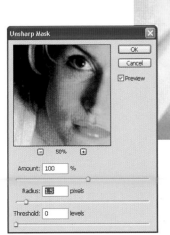

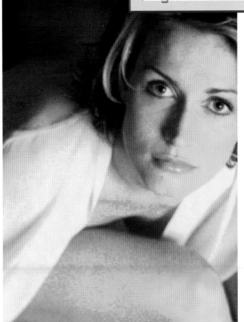

149

Revitalizing faded photographs

When breathing life into photographs faded by time, it's important to assess what specific problems need to be addressed. The common problems associated with fading are reduced contrast, lightening or darkening, and either desaturated colors or a color cast. We've dealt with all of these already—in fact, tackling an aged photo uses the same techniques used when correcting any photo in need of adjustment.

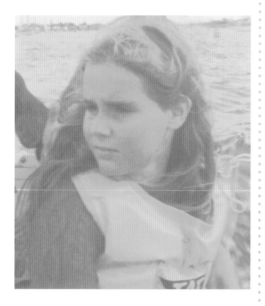

Fixing color and contrast

This photo has suffered as a result of sun exposure: it's faded, and has an orange cast that suffuses the entire image.

1 The first thing to deal with is the poor contrast. We could use Auto Contrast or Auto Levels, not to mention Levels or Curves, but in this case we simply duplicate the background layer and change the new layer's blend mode to Multiply. The contrast is improved, but we still have a major color problem to deal with.

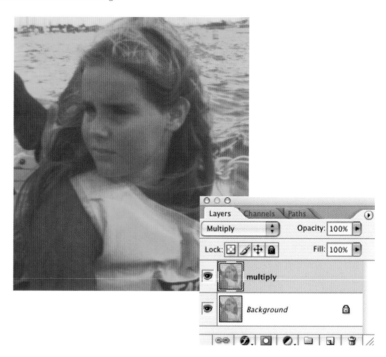

2 The best answer to any problem is the most economical method that gets a great result. For this image, that means Curves. Using a Curves adjustment layer gives us flexibility to fine-tune the result if necessary. Click the Adjustment Layer icon at the bottom of the Layers palette, and choose Curves.

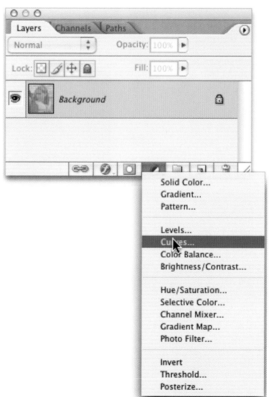

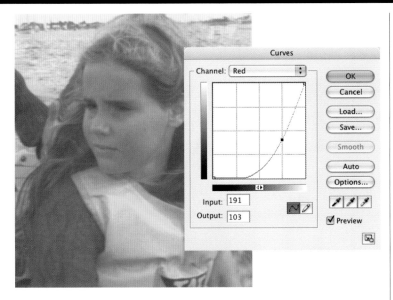

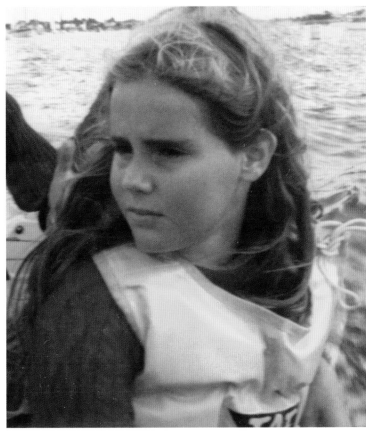

3 We'll tackle the color problems first, the most obvious being the abundance of red. Choose the Red channel from the drop-down and drag the curve downwards. Take it easy, and get a feel for how much adjustment is required. If you drag too much you will see a green cast appearing, so drag until the green starts to creep in then reverse the drag to get to the optimum point.

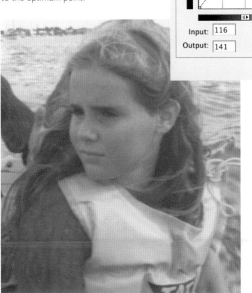

4 Now go straight to the Blue channel. Take a look at the water and the red sweater. Both show too much yellow. Drag the Blue channel's curve upwards to minimize this and strengthen the blue. Once again you will know when you've gone too far, as the blue will become too dominant. Now the colors look more natural and we don't need to adjust the green curve at all.

5 Let's deal with the low contrast (this will saturate the colors further and really revitalize the image). Choose the RGB composite channel from the drop-down. We are going to apply a Contrast curve. Reproduce the curve as shown in the example, then click OK to confirm all the settings. Finally the picture looks more lifelike. The great benefit of having used an Adjustment Layer is that you can go back into the settings and tweak them at a later time, if you decide you want a different look.

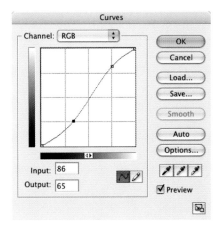

Recreating damaged areas

Photographs that have become worn with age or damaged through handling or poor storage can still be revitalized, depending on the degree of damage and the subject matter. Obviously, even Photoshop can't add a missing head back onto a portrait without another image to act as donor for a "transplant," but if the damage is limited and similar elements exist in the image, we have every chance of making a seamless restoration.

This photograph taken during a family vacation in Spain has suffered a tear and the missing piece has been lost over the years. It has also been creased in the bottom right corner, leaving a white line through the photographic emulsion. I began by scanning the image, trying to keep the torn edges as flat as possible. To minimize the amount of patching up required, we can use the missing area as the basis for a clipping mask.

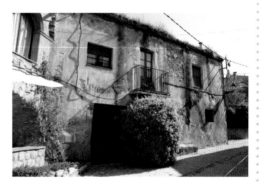

Using clipping masks and Clone Stamp

1 Use the Magic Wand to select the main part of the white torn area. The selection needs to be a little bigger than the tear to avoid showing any pale edges later. Go to **Select > Modify > Expand**, and enter 2 as the value. Press Ctrl/Cmd + J to copy and paste the selection to a new layer, then name the new layer "clipping mask."

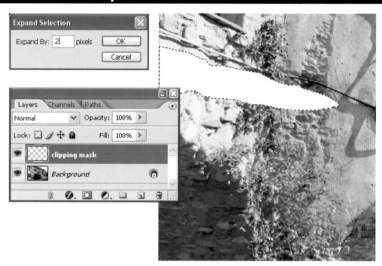

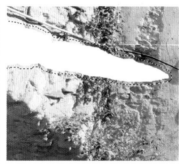
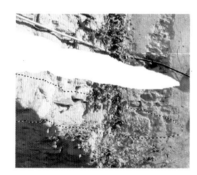

2 Using your original selection, go to **Select > Modify > Expand**, and this time enter a value of 10. This gives you a larger area to work with. Drag this selection to the part of the image which you will duplicate to repair the damaged area.

3 Activate the background layer and press Ctrl/Cmd + J again to copy the selection to its own layer, called "patch." Drag the patch layer above the clipping mask layer, then move the copy of the building over the tear.

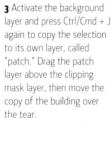
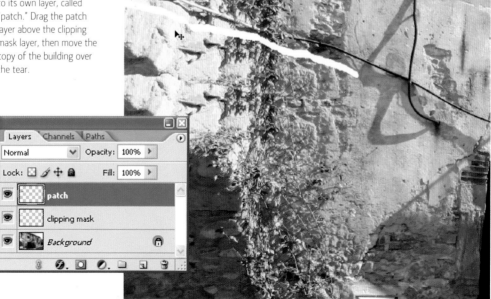

152

4 Now we just need to make a clipping mask between the two layers. Activate the patch layer and press Ctrl/Cmd + G. The layer can now be positioned as desired. Try to line up any obvious areas of color or shadow to make it look as seamless as possible.

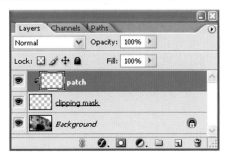

6 The crease in the corner can be fixed quickly by cloning a selection taken from the pixels immediately adjacent to the damaged area. Hold down Alt/Opt+ Ctrl/Cmd and click on the selection. When the cursor is dragged downward, a clone of the selected area neatly repairs the damage.

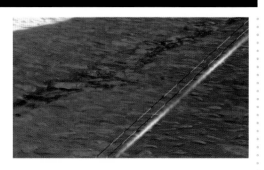

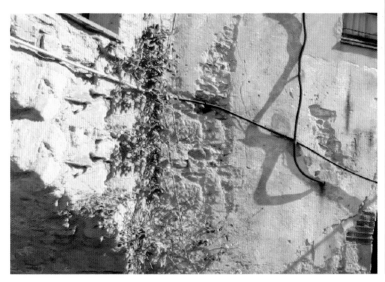

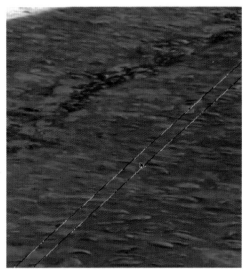

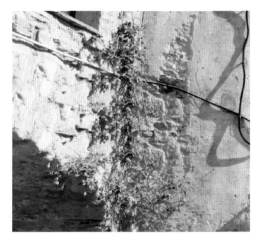

7 The newly repaired image can now replace the damaged original in the family photo album.

5 The area to the right of the window shows an obvious repetition of the stonework directly below it. To solve this problem, create a new layer at the top of the stack called "new stone." Using the Clone Stamp, copy pixels from the surrounding stonework on the background layer to the new stone layer. In this example the irregularity of the stonework has helped to produce a convincing result.

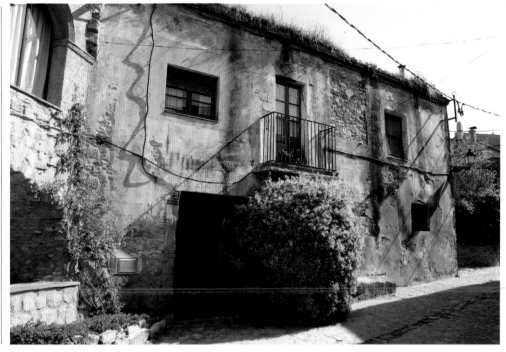

Antique effects

Having just spent several pages explaining how to make an old image look new, we're now going to look at making a new image look old. Why? Because, while the passing years are anything but kind to the printed image, there can be a unique beauty in this aging process. Golden hues and distressed textures can add a poignant tone to an image.

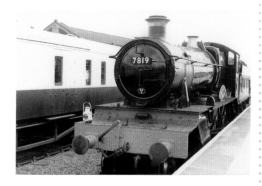

Distressing your images

1 The image we are using here is overexposed, but that's fine for this purpose, as we are looking for a washed-out look. Naturally, an image depicting something that is at least 60 years old adds credibility to the final effect. The first step is to lose all the color and create a brownish tint reminiscent of sepia. Press Ctrl/Cmd + U (or choose **Image>Adjustments>Hue Saturation**). Check the Colorize box and apply the settings shown.

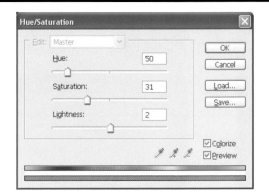

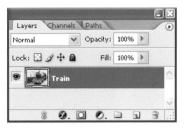

2 Fading is one of the key characteristics of aging photos and an easy one to replicate in Photoshop. Double-click the background layer to convert it to an ordinary layer. Naming it would be a good idea as we will be creating several layers.

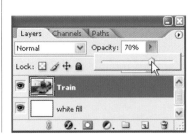

3 You now have two options: work with the overall opacity of the image or else change the image's histogram by using Levels. To try the opacity option, create a new layer, fill it with white, and position it below the train layer. Click on the train layer and change the Opacity setting to 70%. The amount of opacity you will use depends on the effect you are trying to create. Be careful not to lose too much detail by making the opacity too low.

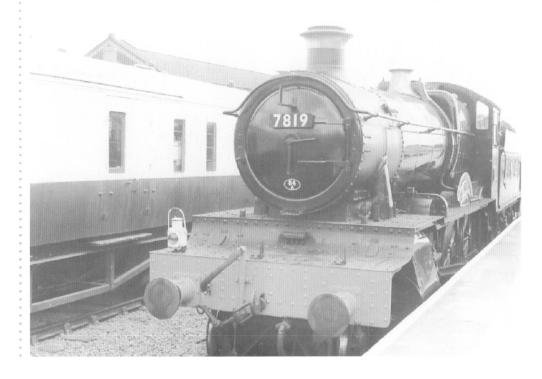

154

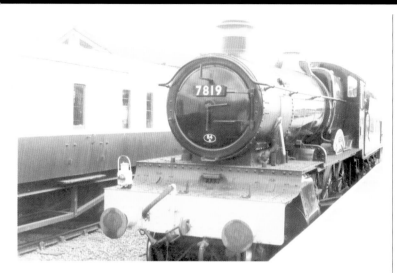

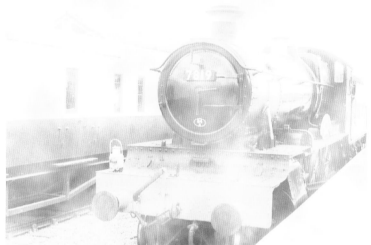

4 You can also achieve this effect by using the Levels function to change the histogram of the image. Press Ctrl/Cmd +L to bring up Levels. Drag the gray and white markers to the left, as shown. This further over-exposes our already over-exposed image, and has a destructive effect that—this time—works in our favor.

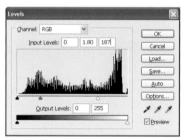

5 To create an even more convincing aging effect, create a new layer above the train layer and name it "clouds." Set up the Foreground and Background colors with a light and dark brown. I'm using R220 G214 B187 for the foreground and R135 G124 B84 for the background.

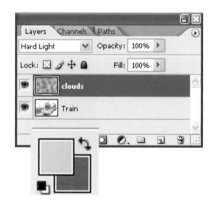

6 Go to **Filter > Render > Clouds** to apply the colors to the clouds layer. Change the blend mode of the clouds layer to Hard Light and we now have the start of a patchy effect.

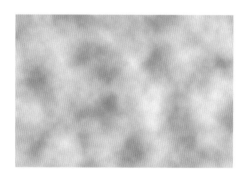

7 Create a new layer above the clouds layer filled with the same pale tan color. Name the layer "noise." Go to **Filter > Noise > Add noise.** Set the Distribution to Uniform, the Amount to 13%, and check the Monochromatic box.

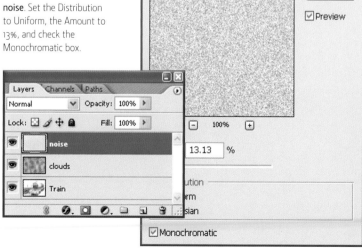

155

Antique effects

Distressing your images continued

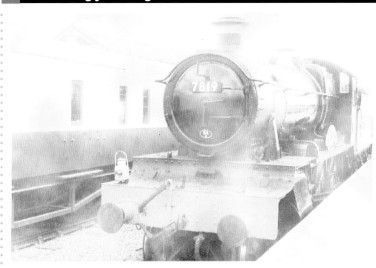

8 Change the noise layer's blend mode to Color Burn. The image should now be starting to look suitably faded, stained, and discolored.

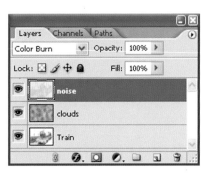

COMPOSITE LAYERS

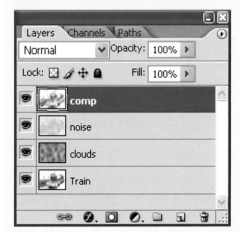

Composite Layers are created by pressing Ctrl/Cmd + Alt + Shift +E. This pastes all the visible layers in a document into a new layer at the top of the layers stack. You can continue to work on this layer with all effects combined and retain the ability to make edits to the other layers at a later time if necessary.

9 If you study a number of very old photos you will often see regular patterns or lines as a result of chemicals, storage, paper degradation or atmospheric conditions. We can replicate this effect, but first we need to combine all our layers together without merging them (we don't want to lose the ability to make changes later). We do this by creating a composite layer. Make a new layer at the top of the layer stack called "comp."

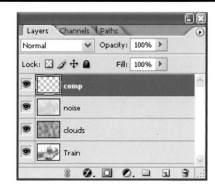

10 Make sure all the layers are visible and press Ctrl/ Cmd + Alt + Shift + E. This rather long "short cut" copies and pastes all the visible layers into a new layer at the top of the stack. We can now continue to work on this new layer with all our effects combined and still have the ability to make edits to the other layers at a later time, if necessary.

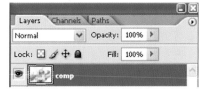

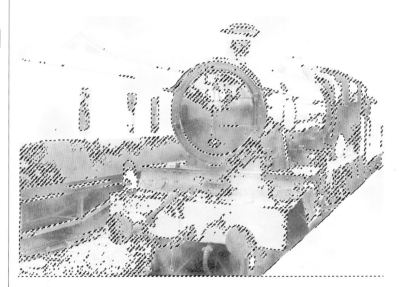

11 Go to the Channels palette and Ctrl/Cmd + Click the Blue channel. This channel has the most contrast and gives us a good random selection.

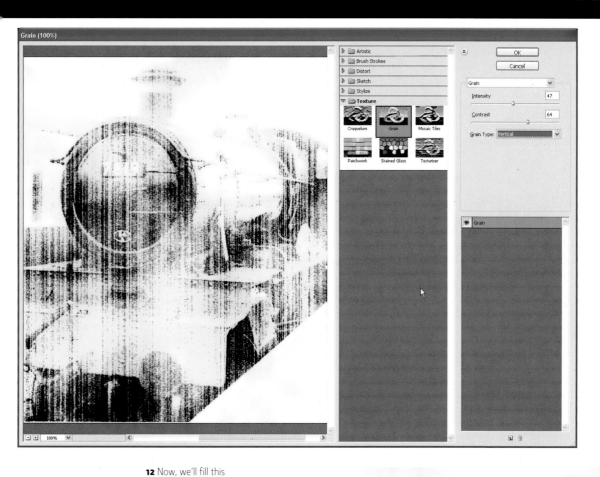

12 Now, we'll fill this selection with a lined pattern. Make sure the composite layer is active and go to **Filter** > **Texture** > **Grain**. Select Vertical as the Grain Type, and set the Intensity to 47 and the Contrast to 64. The final image now has a strong distressed look, with the strains of half a century appearing in just a few short minutes.

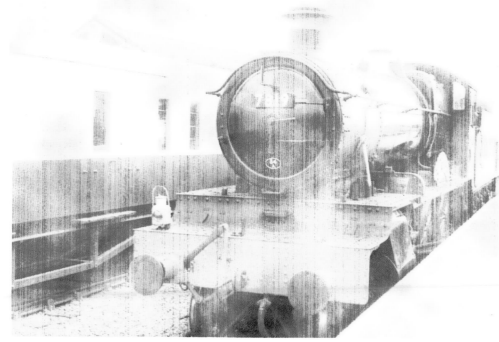

PHOTO COMPOSITING TECHNIQUES

Making selections from channels

Using the Extract command with the History palette

Fine-tuning composites

Making selections from channels

The spindly branches of this tree would make an excellent study in silhouette against a striking sunset, but making a good selection of those intricate fine twigs would test the power of Photoshop and its selection tools—not to mention anyone's patience. A manual selection would be tortuous, and even the Magic Wand and Color Range selector pose problems. Luckily, there is an alternative, using channels.

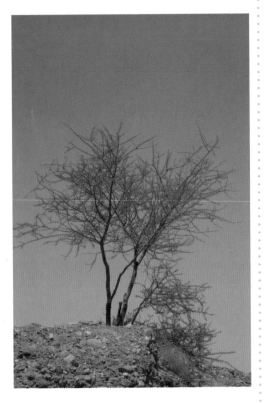

Complex composites made easy

1 The secret is to find a channel that offers plenty of contrast between subject and background. Go to the Layers palette and click the Channels tab, then click each channel in turn to asses the contrast. In this image the Blue channel is the best candidate. We don't want to edit the blue information, so duplicate and rename the blue channel. This duplicate channel is where we will do all the work.

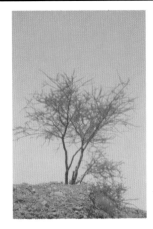

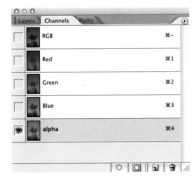

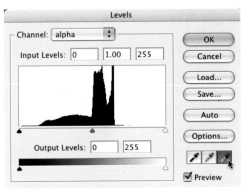

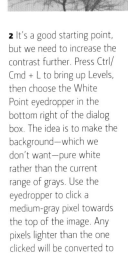

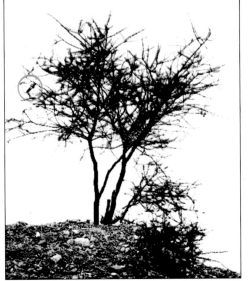

2 It's a good starting point, but we need to increase the contrast further. Press Ctrl/ Cmd + L to bring up Levels, then choose the White Point eyedropper in the bottom right of the dialog box. The idea is to make the background—which we don't want—pure white rather than the current range of grays. Use the eyedropper to click a medium-gray pixel towards the top of the image. Any pixels lighter than the one clicked will be converted to pure white.

3 Choose the Black Point eyedropper and click on a dark gray pixel from within the tree branches. This will make any pixels darker than the clicked pixel convert to pure black, creating the stark contrast that we need.

4 Depending on which pixel you clicked on, you may find some of the background areas that used to be white have now turned gray. Remove this by painting over it in white.

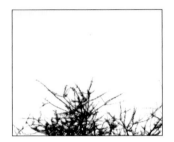

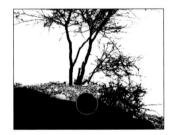

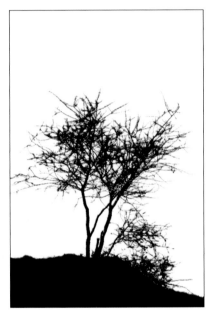

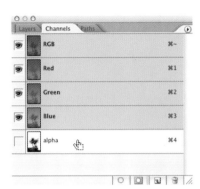

5 We'll keep the earth in which the tree is planted part of the selection. Use a black brush and paint out the earth area. The channel should now look like this:

6 Our work on the Alpha channel is finished—all we do now is to load it as a selection. First, click the RGB composite channel so we can see the color image again. Now, press and hold the Ctrl/Cmd key and click on the Alpha channel to load it.

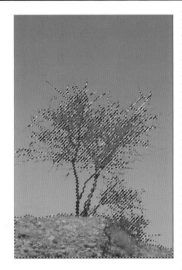

7 Click the Layer tab to return to the Layers palette. The marching ants show the initial selection, but it needs inverting. Go to **Select > Inverse** (Ctrl/Cmd + Shift + I).

8 Open the sunset image, which will provide the new background. Return to the Tree document, and, as the tree is already selected, use the Move tool to drag it from its document into the Sunset document and position it in place. Sadly, one thing gives the game away: the blue "ghosting" surrounding the tree. The tree's original background was blue, and that blue light reflected from the tree becomes an integral part of the tree. To fix the problem we need to employ some advanced compositing techniques (see page 164).

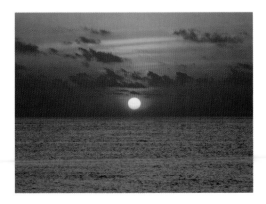

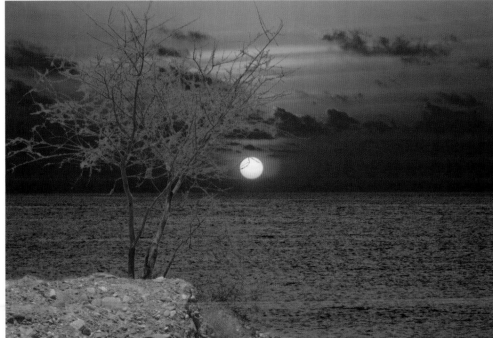

Using the Extract command with the History palette

Cutting objects out from their original backgrounds can be a laborious task, unless the objects are well-defined or there is a clear contrast between the object and the background. The difficulty of this operation has given rise to a number of third-party plug-ins to automate the process, but Adobe adopted these functions into Photoshop's Extract tool. While the Extract tool on its own is extremely useful, it is even more effective when used in conjunction with the History palette and History brush.

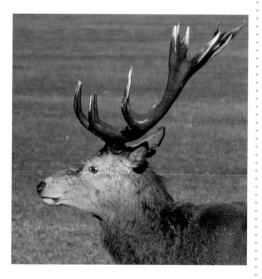

162

Isolating difficult subjects

1 In this example, parts of the deer are particularly difficult to isolate from the background because the texture of the grass is so similar. Using the Extract command will make what would be a very tedious job far easier. Go to **Filter > Extract.** Using the Edge Highlighter, start to outline the deer, changing the size of the brush as necessary.

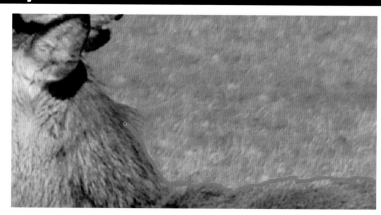

2 In some areas—as around the ears—the edge is well-defined. Enable the Smart Highlighting checkbox in these areas. It will automatically apply just enough paint to cover the edge, thereby helping to maintain a clean extraction.

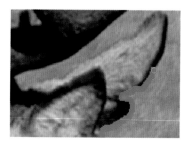
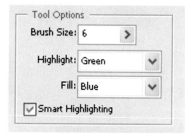

3 Continue to paint until you have a complete green border outlining the deer, making sure there are no gaps. Once that's done, select the Paintbucket and click anywhere within the green border to fill it.

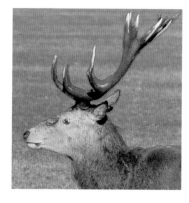
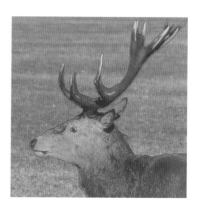

4 At this stage, you can click the Preview button to see how the extraction will look. Here, you can see some ragged edges in places. That's where my highlighting was a little too heavy or not quite accurate enough. I have done this intentionally to demonstrate how the History palette and brush can be used to backtrack after an extraction has been made. Click OK to confirm the extraction.

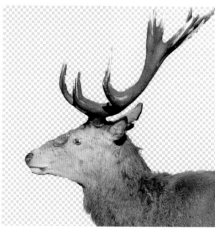

5 Open the History palette if it's not already open (**Window** > **History**) and click the New Snapshot icon at the bottom. We now have two snapshots of the image: the original, which was there from the beginning, called "deer.psd;" and the new one, which I have named "extraction." The brush icon next to the original snapshot tells us that this is the active snapshot.

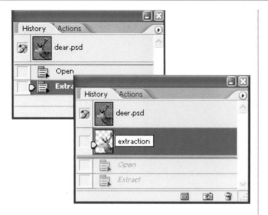

6 We can now use the History brush to put back any parts of the deer that have inadvertently been removed during extraction. Select the History brush from the toolbox and start to paint over any areas where parts of the deer have been removed by mistake. The bottom of the image is the largest area that needs correcting. As you paint, you are taking pixels from the original snapshot, which is currently enabled.

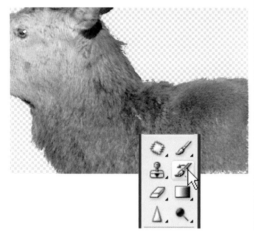

7 This technique can also be used to paint pixels from the new snapshot we made. I've inadvertently painted back too much from the original snapshot on the deer's chest, so I am going to reverse the process. Enable the extraction snapshot in the History palette by clicking the gray box to its left. Paint over the affected area. You are now adding pixels from the snapshot we created immediately after the extraction.

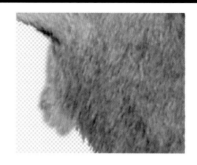

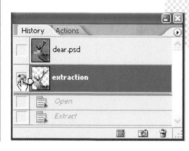

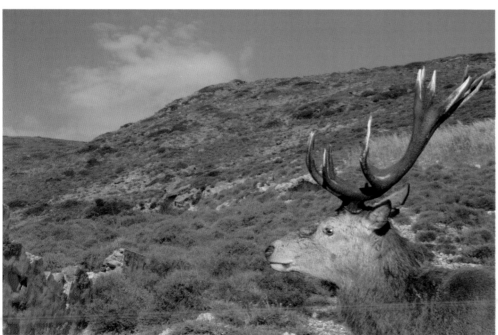

8 Using History in conjunction with the Extract filter provides a whole new level of versatility to an already powerful tool. The final image shows the extracted and cleaned-up deer placed into a more interesting and characteristic landscape. You might agree with me that although the extraction has worked well, the deer doesn't look entirely natural in the new scene. We're going to cover this next (see page 165).

Fine-tuning composites

erhaps you've spent a couple of hours using all of your skill and know-how to cut an object out of the background so you can paste it into a new image. Now you have an object with a razor-sharp edge that's guaranteed to sit seamlessly in its new environment. However, after you've pasted it in, it just doesn't look right. You can't quite put your finger on the reason why. If this sounds like a scenario you sometimes find yourself in, read on.

Method 1: **Layer Blend Modes**

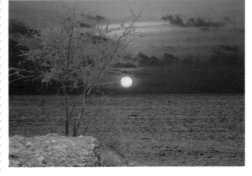

1 The first image comes from our project on making difficult selections using channels (see page 160). The blue halo around the tree we've just pasted into the sunset scene is the result of the blue light in the original image. And, because of the position of the sun in the new image, we'd expect to see the tree and the earth in silhouette, so we have some work to do here.

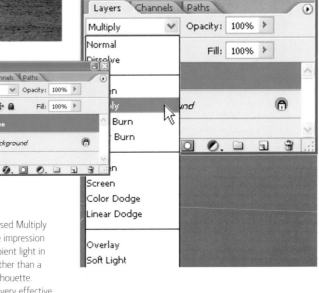

2 One of the quickest and easiest ways to create a silhouette effect for the tree is to use Layer Blend Modes. At present, the tree is on the top layer. With the tree layer active, click the Blend Modes drop-down box. Multiply, Color Burn, or Linear Burn can all be used—with subtle variations in the result—to successfully silhouette the tree.

3 Here, we used Multiply to create the impression of some ambient light in the earth, rather than a fully black silhouette. The result is very effective, even though it required very little work to achieve.

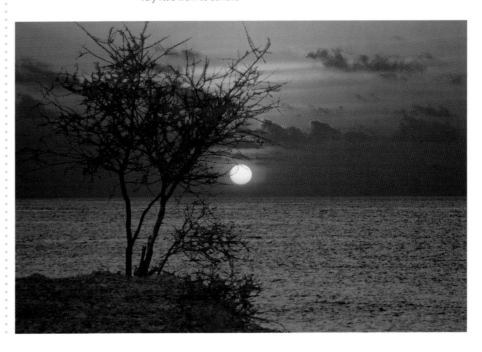

164

1 We can apply the same principle using a manual tool—the advantage being that you can judge which areas need and get the most treatment. Choose the Burn tool from the Toolbox, set the Range to Midtones and the Exposure to a fairly low percentage.

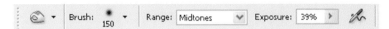

2 Use the Burn tool as you would an ordinary brush. Use multiple clicks to gradually build up the desired degree of darkness. Heavy strokes at high Exposure levels cause a solid black to build up, making the image look false. Leaving some of the foreground and tree bark relatively light allows some of the original detail to come through.

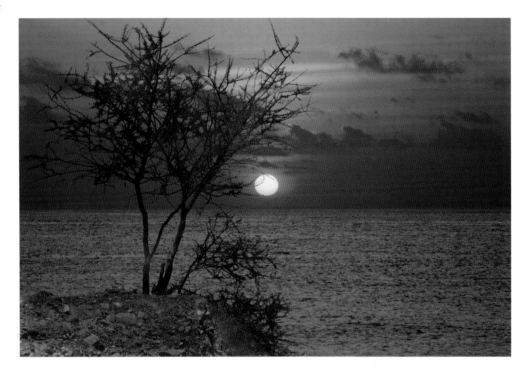

TIP

In this example, the mismatch is obvious. To cover the joins, we can apply several techniques. Blurring the background slightly helps to create a more realistic sense of depth. Selecting the deer from the top layer and blurring a border selection (see page 162) helps match it in to the background. Finally, applying Levels, Curves or Color Balance adjustments, you can ensure the layers match more evenly in tone and color. We'll cover these things in more detail on the next spread.

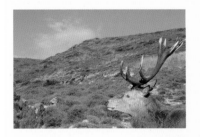

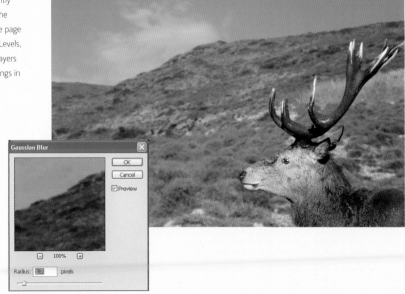

Fine-tuning composites

Method 3: **Advanced compositing techniques**

1 The man on the ladder has been composited with a new layer into the sandy rocks image. Some of the same problems exist as in the previous examples. Colors don't match, there are varying degrees of focus, and there is a slight fringe around the man in certain areas.

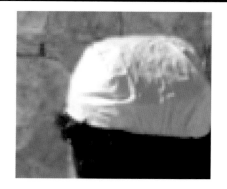

2 Let's deal with the sharpness problem first. In more extreme cases, it might be advisable to either sharpen or blur one of the layers, but in this image the problem isn't clarity as much as contrast. A simple Levels adjustment is all that is required. The sandy rocks on the background layer suffer from low contrast compared with a quite strong contrast on the man layer. Make a Levels adjustment to the background layer, using the settings shown.

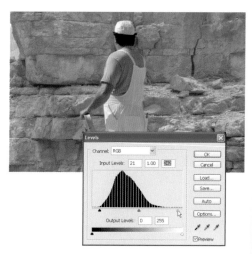

3 The blue fringe around the man is more noticeable in some places than others. The areas around his hair and under his forearm show up the most. To remove this, go to **Layer > Matting > Defringe**. Apply a Width of 1 pixel.

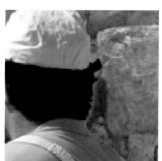

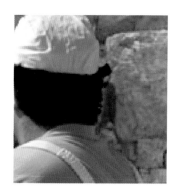

4 One negative aspect of defringing is the fact that it can give the layer a "cutout" appearance. Indeed, any composited layers, even those which have been well-selected and extracted from their original backgrounds can suffer from this problem. The edges look too sharp. The best remedy for this is a border selection. First, load the selection from the man layer. Keep the Ctrl/Cmd key pressed and click the man layer in the layer palette.

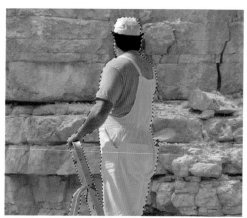

5 Go to **Select> Modify> Border**. Apply a value of 2. This enables us to blur the thin area within the border selection, thereby softening the cutout effect. Use Gaussian blur with a Radius of 1.0. The same area around the baseball cap can now been seen with a smoother edge. This process is effectively like applying anti-aliasing to the layer.

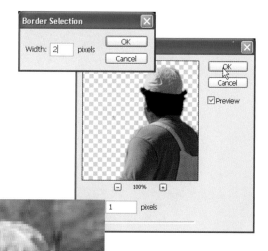

6 The image is starting to look more natural, but the main problem remaining is the difference in color between the two layers. The man has a blue cast which is particularly noticeable in the white of his overalls and cap. To fix this, select the man layer, then go to **Image > Adjustments > Match Color**. Go to the bottom half of the dialog box and select the current document and the background layer from the drop-down. This denotes the background layer as the one from which the calculations will be made.

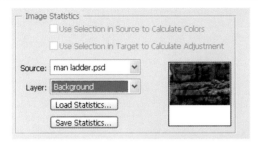

7 The top half of the dialog box tells us which layer is the target layer and provides sliders for increasing or reducing the color effect. The settings shown render a flat brown cast over the man layer.

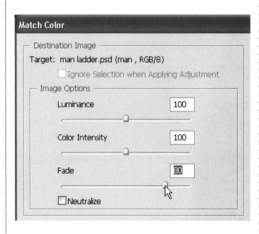

8 Drag the Fade slider to 80 to reduce the strength of the adjustment. The Luminance slider adjusts Lightness and Color Intensity adjusts color saturation. If an unwelcome color cast is generated, check the neutralize checkbox.

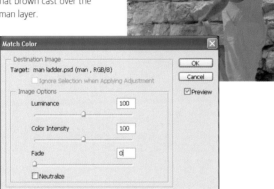

9 If necessary, the Burn tool can be used to darken any edge areas that are still too light. Use the Dodge tool if any areas need lightening.

Glossary

Adjustment layer A specialized layer that can be handled as a conventional layer, but designed to enact effects on layers below it in the image "stack." These include changes to levels, contrast, and color, plus gradients and other effects. These changes do not permanently affect the pixels underneath, so by masking or removing the adjustment layer, you can easily remove the effect from part or all of an image with great ease. You can also return and change the parameters of an adjustment layer at a later stage.

Alpha channel A specific channel used to store transparency information. Alpha channels can be used to store and control selections and masks.

Aperture The opening behind the camera lens through which light passes on its way to the CCD or film.

Artifact A visible flaw in a digital image, usually taking the form of colored blocks or a noticeable fringe.

Black point An adjustable point beneath the histogram in the Levels tool which can be used to define the darkest tone in an image (beneath which all tones will be set to black).

Blending mode In Photoshop, individual layers can be blended with those underneath, rather than simply overlaying them at full opacity. Blending modes control the ways in which the layers interact, enacting changes on one layer using the color information in the other. The result is a new color based on the original color and the nature of the blend.

Brightness The relative lightness or darkness of a color, measured as a percentage from 0% black up to 100% white.

Burn A method of darkening areas in a photographic print by selective masking. Photoshop simulates this digitally.

Channels In Photoshop, a color image is usually composed of three or four separate single-color images, called channels. In standard RGB mode, the Red, Green, and Blue channels will each contain a monochromatic image representing the parts of the image that contain that color. In a CMYK image, the channels will be Cyan, Magenta, Yellow, and Black. Individual channels can be manipulated in much the same way as the composite image.

Clipping Limiting an image or artwork to within the bounds of a particular area.

Clipping group A stack of image layers that produce an image or effect that is a net composite of the constituents. For example, where the base layer is a selection shape (say, an ellipse), the next layer a transparent texture, and the top layer a pattern, the clipping group would produce a textured pattern in the shape of an ellipse.

Color cast A bias in a color image, either intentionally introduced or the undesirable consequence of a mismatch between a camera's white balance and lighting. For example, tungsten lighting may create a warm yellow cast, or daylight scenes shot outdoors with the camera's color balance set for an indoor scene may have a cool blue cast.

Color temperature A measure of the composition of light, defined as the temperature—measured in degrees Kelvin—to which a pure black object would need to be heated to produce a particular color of light. A tungsten lamp has a color temperature of around 2,900K, while the temperature of direct sunlight is around 5,000K.

Color wheel The complete spectrum of visible colors represented as a circular diagram.

Complementary colors Any pair of colors directly opposite each other on a color wheel. When you heighten the effect of one color, you lessen the effect of its opposite.

Contrast The degree of difference between adjacent tones in an image, from the lightest to the darkest.

Crop To trim or mask an image so that it fits a given area or so that unwanted portions can be discarded.

Curves A Photoshop tool for precise control of tonal relationships, contrast, and color.

Default The standard setting or action used by an application without any intervention from the user.

Depth of field The range in front of the lens in which objects will appear in clear focus. With a shallow depth of field, only objects at or very near the focal point will be in focus and foreground or background objects will be blurred. Depth of field can be manipulated in-camera for creative effect, and Photoshop's new Lens Blur filter enables you to replicate it in postproduction.

Dialog An on-screen window in an application used to enter or adjust settings or complete a step-by-step procedure.

Dodge A method of lightening areas in a photographic print by selective masking. Photoshop simulates this digitally.

Drag To move an item or selection across the screen, by clicking and holding the cursor over it, then moving the mouse with the button still pressed.

Eyedropper A tool used to define the foreground and background colors in the Tools palette, either by clicking on colors that appear in an image, or in a specific color palette dialog box. Eyedroppers are also used to sample colors for Levels, Curves, and Color Range processes.

Feather An option used to soften the edge of a selection that has been moved or otherwise manipulated, in order to hide the seams between the selected area and the pixels that surround it.

Fill A Photoshop operation which covers a defined area with a particular color, gradient, or texture.

Gradient Tool permitting the creation of a gradual blend between two colors within a selection. There are several types, including linear, radial, and reflected gradients.

Grayscale An image or gradient made up of a series of 256 gray tones covering the entire gamut between black and white.

Handle An icon used in an image-editing application to manipulate an effect or selection. These usually appear on screen as small black squares.

Hard light A blending mode that creates an effect similar to directing a bright light on the subject, emphasizing contrast and exaggerating highlights.

High key An image comprised predominantly of light tones.

Histogram A graphic representation of the distribution of brightness values in an image, normally ranging from black at the left-hand vertex to white at the right. Analysis of the shape of the histogram can be used to evaluate tonal range.

Image size The size of an image, in terms of linear dimensions, resolution, or simple file size. In Photoshop, we mainly talk about image size by describing horizontal and vertical dimensions (e.g., 1,280 x 1,024), qualified by the resolution (e.g., 72ppi).

Interpolation A procedure used when resizing a bitmap image to maintain resolution. When the number of pixels is increased beyond the number of pixels existing in the image, interpolation creates new pixels to fill in the gaps by comparing the values of the adjacent pixels and estimating the color content of any new pixels.

Layer A feature used to produce composite images by suspending image elements on separate overlays. Once these layers have been created, they can be re-ordered, blended, and their transparency (opacity) may be altered.

Layer effects A series of useful preset effects that can be applied to the contents of a layer. Examples include drop shadows, embossing, and color tone effects.

Layer mask A mask that can be applied to elements of an image in a particular layer, defining which pixels will or will not be visible or affect pixels underneath.

Low key A photographic image consisting of predominantly

dark tones, either as a result of lighting, processing, or digital image editing.

Mask In conventional photography, a material used to protect part or all of an image from adjustments in the darkroom. Image-editing applications feature a digital equivalent, used to control the effects of adjustments or manipulation and to protect specific areas or elements.

Midtones The range of tonal values that exist between the darkest and lightest tones in an image.

Mixed lighting Lighting in a shot illuminated by several different sources with different color temperatures, which may prove a challenge for a camera's white balance setting. An example would be an interior scene lit with tungsten lights along with daylight coming in through a window.

Motion blur In photography, the blurring effect caused by movement of objects within the frame during the exposure of the shot. Photoshop contains filters to replicate motion blur.

Multiply A blending mode that uses the pixels of one layer to multiply those below. The resulting color is always darker, except where white appears on an upper layer.

Noise A random pattern of small spots on a digital image, usually caused by the inadequacies of digital camera CCDs in low-light conditions. Photoshop's Noise filters can add or remove noise from an image.

Opacity In a layered Photoshop document, the degree of transparency that each layer of an image has in relation to the layer beneath. As the opacity is lowered, the layer beneath shows through.

Overlay A blending mode that retains black and white in their original forms, but darkens dark areas and lightens light areas.

PPI Pixels per inch. The most common unit of resolution, describing how many pixels are contained within a single square inch of an image.

Quick Mask A feature designed to rapidly create a mask around a selection. By switching to Quick Mask mode, the user can paint and erase the mask using simple brushstrokes.

Resampling Changing the resolution of an image, either by removing pixels (lowering resolution) or adding them by interpolation (increasing resolution).

Resolution The degree of quality, definition, or clarity with which an image is reproduced or displayed on screen or on the printed page. The higher the resolution, the more pixels are contained within a given area, and the greater the detail captured.

Screen A blending mode that calculates the inverse of one layer and multiplies this with the values of pixels below, bleaching colors except where the color is black. In photographic terms, it's the equivalent of printing a positive image from two negatives sandwiched together.

Soft light A blending mode with an effect similar to Overlay, but with a gentler result.

Specular highlight An intense highlight, often resulting from the reflection of an extremely bright light source such as the sun or a lighting reflector. Specular highlights are plentiful in photographs of highly reflective surfaces such as glass or highly polished metal.

White balance A setting used in a digital photo or video camera to compensate for the varying color temperatures of different forms of lighting. A tungsten preset, for example, will adjust for the amount of yellow light given off by tungsten lighting.

White point An adjustable point beneath the histogram in the Levels tool which can be used to define the lightest tone in an image (above which all tones will be set to white).

Index

Further reading

Digital photography and digital imaging have spawned communities, websites, and a number of excellent journals, all of which provide useful sources of advice, tips, and information for the Photoshop user.

Magazines

CaptureUser
www.captureuser.com
U.S. magazine that is the official publication for Nikon Capture users

Computer Arts
www.computerarts.co.uk
U.K. publication (though widely available worldwide) specializing in all aspects of digital art, including Photoshop

Digital Camera
www.dcmag.co.uk
U.K. magazine with reviews and tutorials on digital photography and Photoshop

Digital Photo Effects
www.dcmag.co.uk
Sister title to Digital Camera, specializing in digital image-editing using Photoshop and similar packages

Digital PhotoPro
www.digitalphotopro.com
U.S. magazine covering advanced technology and creativity

Layers Magazine
www.layersmagazine.com
U.S. magazine dedicated to Adobe technologies (including Photoshop)

PCPhoto
pcphotomag.com
U.S. magazine covering digital photography and imaging

PDN
www.pdnonline.com
Acronym for "Photo District News"; U.S.-based magazine for shooting pros and serious students

PHOTOgraphic
www.photographic.com
US digital photography magazine, containing some tips and tutorials for Photoshop users

Photo Techniques
www.phototechmag.com/
Magazine aimed at the serious digital photographer, with solid tips on photo retouching

Photoshop User
www.photoshopuser.com
The publication of the U.S.-based National Association of Photoshop Professionals (NAPP)

Rangefinder
www.rangefindermag.com
U.S.-based magazine for professional photographers

Websites

Adobe
www.adobe.com
The home of Photoshop, and a useful source of support, downloads, and training files

CreativeCow
www.creativecow.net
Useful forums for design professionals, with a lively following of Photoshop users

Creativepro.com
www.creativepro.com
News and resources for creative professionals

DesignerToday
www.designertoday.com
A wealth of tutorials on design applications, including many on Photoshop

Digital Photography
www.digitalphotography.org
News and product reviews for digital photographers

Imaging Resource
www.imaging-resource.com
Imaging-related news and reviews

O'Reilly Digital Media
http://digitalmedia.oreilly.com/
News, features, and links to essential books for digital photographers and Photoshop artists

Photoshop Café
www.photoshopcafe.com
Numerous tutorials covering every aspect of Photoshop

Planet Photoshop
www.planetphotoshop.com
Comprehensive portal for all things Photoshop

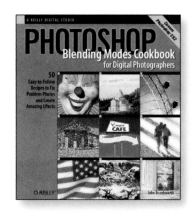
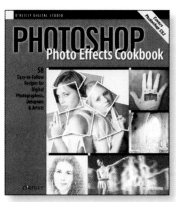
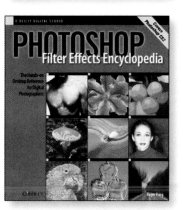

◆ INSPIRATION

THE DESIGNER'S NOTEBOOK SERIES from O'Reilly presents a collection of concise, visually stunning lessons designed to inspire and instruct illustrators, graphic designers, and digital photographers of all levels. Reflecting the best in the world of digitally created images, these books offer eye-candy, artistic inspiration, and incomparable technical guidance. Look for them at your favorite bookstore. For more information, visit *www.oreilly.com/go/pum3*.

Translated into English and available in the US for the first time, the Designer's Notebooks showcase the breathtaking work of top French graphic artists and digital graphics professionals.

Assembling Panoramic Photos
A Designer's Notebook
ISBN: 0-596-00975-5, 96 pages, $24.95US/$34.95 CAN

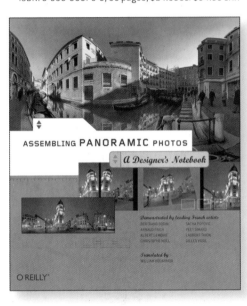

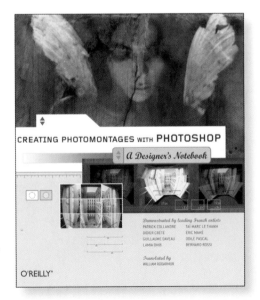

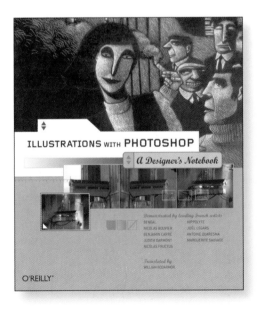

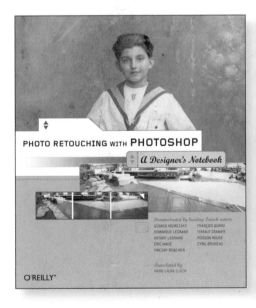

Creating Photomontages with Photoshop
A Designer's Notebook
ISBN: 0-596-00858-9, 96 pages
$24.95US/$34.95 CAN

Illustrations with Photoshop
A Designer's Notebook
ISBN: 0-596-00859-7, 96 pages
$24.95US/$34.95 CAN

Photo Retouching with Photoshop
A Designer's Notebook
ISBN: 0-596-00860-0, 96 pages
$24.95US/$34.95 CAN